Preaching Priest

Preaching Priest

The life of
Martin Boos

Christian Focus Publications Ltd

Published by
Christian Focus Publications Ltd

Tain
Ross-shire

Houston
Texas

1989 Christian Focus Publications Ltd

ISBN 1 871 676 08 8

Foreword

In his ninth pastoral letter, Robert Murray McCheyne gives a chilling impression of the grip which Romanism had on France. He ends his observations on a more hopeful note — "and yet, remember what I used to read to you out of Martin Boos, and remember the saying of the Lord to Elijah. There may be many hidden ones even in Babylon."

The following pages provide confirmation of McCheyne's words. It was through one of these secret ones Martin Boos, himself, came to the light of the gospel. Thereafter, he was to encounter many hitherto unknown sympathisers in his numerous enforced wanderings. Above all, these pages are the record of how, under God, he was himself the means of turning many to righteousness within the Roman fold.

The phrase, "apostolic labours" may trip lightly off the tongue when commending a faithful ministry; but, surely, in application to Martin Boos it is singularly appropriate. Like Paul, he determined to know nothing among men save Jesus Christ and him crucified; like Paul, Boos suffered much from legalistic brethren; like Paul, he was frequently driven from city to city, even from country to country; like Paul, Boos' life was a model of simplicity; he counted not his life dear to himself that he might finish his course with joy.

Whence came this life-long martyrdom? Doubtless, as suggested in this book, he suffered much because his influence and reputation aroused the jealousy of his fellow priests. "Ordinary politics sometimes has its sordid side; politics in Church affairs always has," wrote professor Hermann Bavinck in what must have been a particularly embittered moment.

He suffered, also, because the preaching of the cross brings its own offence. We who are protestants may think with some complacency that the beginning and ending of his afflication stemmed from the fact he remained a Roman Catholic. Salvation by faith, which Boos preached mixes as well with Roman Catholic doctrine as oil with water. We would do well to remember that in Protestant England, earlier in the same century, Whitfield was accused to his bishop for driving fifteen persons mad in his first sermon. That was only the beginning of a persecution which forced him in the end to take to the fields. About the same time, in Protestant Scotland, Boston's "Marrow" — bearing the same message of free grace — had been roundly condemned by the General Assembly.

After all is said and done, however, it is clear that much of the Boos' suffering flowed from the fact that the doctrine of the Council of Trent speaks of infused grace flowing through the sacraments rather than imputed righteousness received by faith as the basis of salvation. Likewise, "works" are given a prominence altogether foreign to the Epistle to the Romans. On trial, Boos appealed to the Word of God and, remarkably enough, was never found guilty of heresy. Not so remarkably, persecution would flare up again when he returned to his parish and preached the requirement of "living faith".

Let the last word be a positive one. Speaking of the R.C. Church in his own time, Samuel Rutherford says, "The Word of God, and so the contract of marriage, is professed among them, and so there is an external active calling there, and the word of the covenant sounding amongst them, and a passive calling, also, because many secretly believe and obey. Many fundamental truths are taught that may beget faith, and so there are true and valid pastoral acts in that Church" [Paul's Presbytery, ch.10]. Had he lived till a century and a half later, Rutherford would have rejoiced to see in the life of Martin Boos a living illustration of his words.

S. Fraser Tallach
Kinlochbervie
Scotland, April 1989

CONTENTS.

———

CHAPTER V.

CHAPTER VI.

CHAPTER VII.

CHAPTER VIII.

CHAPTER IX.

CHAPTER X.

CHAPTER XI.

CHAPTER XII.

CHAPTER XXI.

CHAPTER XXII.

LIFE OF MARTIN BOOS.

CHAPTER I

Birth and Education.

MARTIN BOOS was born December 25; 1762, at
Hulbenried, on the confines of Upper Bavaria
and Suabia. His father was a respectable
farmer, with a stock of twenty cows and four
horses. His mother had sixteen children, of
whom he was the youngest but two. He was
scarcely five years old when both his parents
were carried off, within a fortnight of each
other, by an epidemic which proved fatal to
numbers in that part of the country. They
left twelve orphans, the eldest, a girl of
eighteen ; but He who "feedeth the young
ravens when they cry," provided homes for
them in the families of their nearest relatives,
who divided the orphans amongst them.

On Whit-Monday Martin's eldest sister,
with her little brother on her back, set off on
foot to the city of Augsburg, where they had
an uncle named Koegel, who held the offices
of fiscal and ecclesiastical counsellor. Tired

of her burden, she laid Martin down in a corn-field, and walked on to Augsburg alone. She came back in the course of the afternoon to the corn-field, where Martin had fallen fast asleep, took him to his uncle, and begged him to adopt the child as his own. Her request was granted ; but Martin (as if from a presenti-ment of what he would suffer in that city in after life) entreated that he might go back to Hulbenried. To escape his importunity, his sister, after staying with him two days, rose early in the morning and left him without taking leave : so that he was obliged to remain.

At eight years old he was sent to school. One year after another passed away; and as no complaints were heard from the master, coun-sellor Koegel did not trouble himself to make any inquiries about his nephew's proficiency. At length one day, when Martin asked for the money due for his schooling, his uncle said to him, somewhat sharply, " There it is ! but it is high time for you to leave school, and learn some trade. What would you like to be ?" " I should like to be a clergyman," said Martin. " You a clergyman !" was the reply; " why you have neither brains nor money for that !" This was a sad rebuff to Martin ; but, in a few minutes, his uncle desired him to come to him after dinner that he might take a note to the school-master, to inquire about his pro-ficiency. The old master gave Martin the best of characters, and said that, of all his pupils, he was the most forward in Latin, and it would be a sin and a shame to cut short the studies of so promising a youth. This was the first time that the uncle had heard of Martin's learning Latin : for the little interest he had shown in his progress, rendered the boy fearful of mentioning it to him, lest he should be angry at his aspiring too high for one in his dependent situation. Such apprehensions were, however, ill-founded. Koegel, on reading the master's note, at once said, "Well, since you have so good a character, I am willing to make the trial, and allow you to go on with your studies; but if you slacken your efforts, depend upon it, you shall be a shoemaker, and nothing more."

Martin now entered the school of the Ex-Jesuits in the Gymnasium of St. Salvador. In five years he passed through the lower classes with credit, and then proceeded to study logic in the Lyceum. At the vacation he returned home. His uncle was true to his promise, and had formed a plan for his future course. "Where have you been all this time?" he abruptly exclaimed; and in the same breath, added, "To-morrow you are to set out for the University at Dillengen. Lose no time in getting your certificate from the Ex-Jesuits."- But the Ex-Jesuits, when they found where he was going, refused to give the necessary testimonials, alleging that it was a very dangerous place for young persons. This was owing to their violent prejudices

against several excellent men among the professors, particularly Sailer and Zimmer. They
offered, if he remained at Augsburg, to procure for him a good situation as private
teacher, so that he would be entirely provided
for, be able to study free of expense, and be
quite independent of his uncle's assistance.
When Martin came back with the answer, his
uncle, who was no friend to the Jesuits, was
highly incensed, and said, " Go again, and
tell them to give the certificates, or I shall take
means to compel them." This peremptory
demand was successful, and very favourable
testimonials were given. The next day Martin
proceeded to Dillengen, though the insinuations
of the Jesuits had given him an unfavour-
able impression of the place and the professors. Here he studied philosophy and meta-
physics with ardour ; and, after undergoing an
examination, was permitted to attend the
theological class gratuitously. He returned to
Augsburg at the vacation; and, for the first
time in his life, had the happiness of being
commended by his uncle, in consequence of
the favourable report of the director of the
University.

For four years Martin studied theology,
pastoral duties, moral philosophy, canon law,
and church history. At the beginning of the
first year he passed through the four minor
orders; in the second year, at Easter, he was
made sub-deacon. His studies were inter-
rupted by a fever, from which he recovered

only a week before Whitsuntide. But as his
uncle wished him to be ordained priest in the
autumn, he attended for four days to the spiritual exercises, and then went with the other
candidates to Augsburg. He there acquitted
himself with great credit, and, as his dread of
a failure had been extreme, his joy was proportionably great.

In the autumn he was admitted to priest's
orders. At his first celebration of mass there
were five hundred communicants, besides
thirty-five of the clerical order. This numerous attendance was principally out of
respect to counsellor Koegel, the uncle; and
the old gentleman was so much gratified with
it, that he gave a three days' shooting party.

Martin had still two years to spend at Dillengen, in order to complete his studies. After
that he spent seven weeks in the seminary of
Pfaffenhausen; and when he left that place,
obtained a curacy at Unterthingau, a large
town in Lower Suabia.

CHAPTER II.

Settlement at Unterthingau—Conversion

WHEN Boos entered on his clerical duties at Unterthingau, probably any one who should have ventured to intimate a doubt of his fitness for the office, would have been met by the self-justifying interrogatory, "What lack I yet?" From his earliest years his conduct had been irreproachable; his application to his literary and theological studies had been close and successful; and he was habitually conscientious and devout. Such he was in the eyes of his fellow-men. Yet his heart was not at rest, nor was his mind spiritually enlightened. He could not say with St. Paul, "The life which I now live in the flesh I live by the faith of the Son of God, who loved me, and gave himself for me." He was trying to be his own Saviour, and to find for himself a path to heaven. His good works, mortifications, and fasts, were the sacrifices he offered to God for expiating his sins, and obtaining everlasting life. Let us listen to his own account of himself. In a letter to a friend, written more than twenty years afterwards, dated December 17, 1811, he thus writes:—

"You speak of me as a constant martyr, and so I have been. In early life my sins made me a martyr; for a long time I knew no Saviour from them but myself. And when, at a later period I had found a Saviour, I was martyred by the consistories and Judaizers, who, by threats, disputations, and exile, would have robbed me of my faith and my Saviour; and this tragedy is kept up to the present time. Add to this, Satan, and my own wicked, presumptuous, desponding heart. It is a miracle that I am still alive. I feel myself dreadfully old, though I am hardly fifty. I once took immense pains (I speak as a fact) to be a very pious man. For example, for years together, even in winter, I lay on the cold floor. I scourged myself till I bled again. I fasted and gave my bread to the poor. I spent every hour I could spare in the church or the cemetery. I confessed and took the sacrament almost every week. In short, I gained such a character for piety, that I was appointed prefect of the congregation by the Ex-Jesuits. But what a life I led! The prefect, with all his sanctity, became more and more absorbed in self; melancholy, anxious, and formal. The saint was evermore exclaiming in his heart, ' O wretched man that I am! who shall deliver me?' and no one replied, ' The grace of God, through Jesus Christ our Lord.' No one gave the sick man that spiritual specific, ' The just shall live by faith;' and when I had obtained it, and found

the benefit of it, the whole world, with all its
learning and spiritual authority, would have
persuaded me that I had swallowed poison,
and was poisoning all around me; that I
deserved to be hung, drowned, immured,
banished, or burnt. I know not a more
timorous mortal than myself, and yet, timid
hare as I am, the whole world dreads and
opposes me. Nothing would gratify me more
than to be at rest, unknown, and unrenowned;
but so it is, few are more talked about than I
am in all quarters. Such, in brief, is the
course of my life. When I am dead, give the
world my best wishes and say, the only specific
I can bequeath for its maladies is, ' The just
shall live by faith.' This has cured myself
and others. But if it has no confidence in me
and my prescription, I cannot help it. I tried
as long as other people the notion that a man
can be saved and justified by his own doings;
but I have found in an ancient document that
we are to be justified and saved for Christ's
sake, without our merits, and in this faith I
shall die. If others will not make use of this
bridge, they must wade through the stream;
but let them see to it, that they are not
drowned."

The manner in which he was brought into a
state of evangelical light and freedom is related
in another letter, written in prison at Lintz,
December 3, 1815.

" I rejoice that, after such a lapse of time,
and so many sufferings, you can still believe

that Christ began this work in me, which to the world is so strange and offensive. It commenced in a very simple manner.

"In 1788 or 1789 I visited a sick person, who was respected for her deep humility and exemplary piety. I said to her, 'You will die very peacefully and happily.' 'Why so?' she asked. 'Because you have led,' I replied, 'such a pious and holy life.' The good woman smiled at my words and said, 'If I leave the world relying on my own piety, I am sure I shall be lost. But relying on Jesus my Saviour, I can die in comfort. What a clergyman you are! what an admirable comforter! If I listened to you, what would become of me? How could I stand before the Divine tribunal, where every one must give an account even of her idle words? Which of our actions and virtues would not be found wanting if laid in the Divine balances? No; if Christ had not died for me, if he had not made satisfaction for me, I should have been lost for ever, notwithstanding all my good works and pious conduct. He is my hope, my salvation, and my eternal happiness.'"

Such is the account given by the good man of the beginning of his deep acquaintance with the mystery of the redemption by Jesus Christ. He found instruction where he sought it not. He entered the house of affliction to console without knowing the true consolation. At first he was astounded and ashamed that what he, after all his studies, was ignorant of, should be taught him by a simple-hearted woman on her death-bed. Happily for him, he was humble enough not to reject the truth when conveyed to him by so mean an instrument. It made an indelible impression on his mind, and formed the foundation of his future faith and life.

From this period, Boos received Christ as his Saviour wholly and entirely, and tasted the peace and joy of salvation. But henceforth, he also found how true it is that they "who will live godly in Christ Jesus, shall suffer persecution." He preached salvation by grace, the gift of God, which man must be content to receive as a free and undeserved gift; and to preach such a doctrine in a church where, though the name of Christ was preserved, human works were substituted as the means of salvation, was to shake its very foundations, and to incur the hatred and opposition of its adherents. But he was firm against all their assaults. The Saviour upheld him, and enabled him to "rejoice that he was accounted worthy to suffer for his name's sake."

Of his labours in his first parish, we possess no information except what is contained in a letter from an officer in the Austrian army who, in his boyhood, received religious instruction from Boos. They met again, thirty years afterwards, in Austria. Boos was then persecuted and in prison; but received from his former pupil every attention that affection and gratitude could suggest. "How often have I and my family," says this worthy man, "been grieved that my earliest instructor, Martin Boos, whose whole soul is filled with love, should be so great a sufferer! I recollect how many of my tears he wiped away, when I lived in my boyhood at Unterthingau, where I was born; how unwearied he was day and night in consoling the sick and the afflicted; with what earnestness and affection he taught. and with what zeal he discharged his ministerial duties. I often call to mind the circumstance of his interring my father, and how he gave me his last shilling, and at the same time exhorted me to diligence in my studies."

Thus after the lapse of years Boos met with sympathy and comfort in the hour of trial, as the result of his pious labours and disinterested charity. We are here reminded of the Scripture expression : " Their works do follow them." The officer never forgot the shilling; for, whenever Boos appeared reluctant to accept his kind offices, he was sure to say, " You gave me your last shilling."

CHAPTER III.

Chaplain at Kempten—Canon at Grünenbach—Expulsion—
Curate at Seeg—at Wiggensbach.

AFTER remaining about two years at Unterthingau, Boos was called to Kempten to be
chaplain of the monastery, and, soon after, to
Grünenbach, as canon.   The devotion he
manifested in the pulpit and the confessional,
soon gained him the confidence of the people,
who flocked in crowds to hear him.   All who
were in earnest about religion applied to him
for consolation and instruction, being convinced
that his great aim was to save himself and
those that heard him.   But his popularity
quickly excited the jealousy of the other clergy,
and especially of the dean.   It awakened the
envy of the senior clergy to see that Boos, the
youngest and last elected, had the largest share
of the general confidence and esteem.   So
devoid were they of all honourable feeling, (to
say nothing of Christian integrity,) that during
his absence from his apartment they broke
open his desk, ransacked his papers, and read
his private correspondence.   Thus furnished
with the means of annoying him, they insulted

and ridiculed him at their meals, and did all in their power to embitter his life.

At last he was obliged to quit Grünenbach. He set out, not knowing which way to direct his steps. As he went along, he perceived a thatched cottage at a little distance from the highway. On entering it, he found it empty, and fell on his knees, and poured out his heart before God. Nor were his prayers (as no real prayer can be) in vain. He was conscious of an inward illumination. He beheld Christ as his Mediator and Saviour, as he had never done before. Comfort, peace, and joy, returned to his troubled heart, and he pursued his journey with cheerfulness.

On arriving at Seeg, he met with a kind reception from a venerable clergyman, named Feneburg. Here he was obliged to descend from the dignity of a canon, to be once more a mere curate. But ecclesiastical rank and outward honours were no objects of solicitude to him; his chief concern was the spiritual welfare of the church; and, for himself, a life of faith in Christ. His activity and faithfulness were greater than ever.

The prince abbot of Kempten, hearing of the treatment Boos had met with at Grünenbach, recalled him in 1795, and appointed him to the curacy of the neighbouring parish of Wiggensbach, with the prospect of soon obtaining a living. It was here that Boos became confirmed in the faith, or, to use St. Paul's language, "rooted and built up in Christ."

The reading of the Scriptures, and various religious works, formed his most delightful occupation. After the example of the Saviour, he passed whole nights in prayer and meditation. There was a retired spot in the church, which was always dear to his remembrance. "Behind the high altar at Wiggensbach," he frequently observed to his intimate friends, " I obtained my living faith, and all the gifts and graces which the Lord has granted me. There the Lord manifested to me his full and ever-availing righteousness. There ˙I learned to know his cross, his merits, and his grace." His preaching, combined with his pious and exemplary conduct, made an extraordinary impression, and led many to a knowledge of themselves, and of Jesus Christ. In a spiritual sense, "the blind received their sight, the lame walked, and the lepers were cleansed."

The following hints are a specimen of the advice Boos was wont to give to persons who were inquiring after the way of salvation.

" 1. When, in your own eyes, you are wicked, blind, lame, leprous, troubled, and perplexed, then is the time for you, like the blind and leprous in the gospel, to seek refuge in faith alone. Like the thief on the cross, you must go, just as you are, with all your faults and sins, to ask forgiveness, and seek earnestly the righteousness he has wrought out for you ; and then lay hold of it, even with tears, and joyfully make it your own. For if God has given you to know the misery of sin, it is in order that you may come to seek forgiveness from the Saviour. If he has made you 'poor in spirit,' it is that you may obtain, by faith, the kingdom of heaven, and all the riches which Jesus has merited for you by his sufferings. Come, then, whenever you are sensible of your poverty and sinfulness, and receive 'grace upon grace.' But when you have, by grace, believed—that is, when, through the righteousness of Jesus Christ, you have received the forgiveness of your sins by faith—then you must apply yourself to spiritual improvement, to a course of holy obedience, and the imitation of Jesus Christ. Not as if you could justify yourself by your good works; or as if, by these means, you could gain the forgiveness of your sins. No, you must perform all this out of love and gratitude, because God, for Christ's sake, has already forgiven you, and imparted to you the spirit and mind of Christ, and has freely given you eternal life, with the power to live holily, and to obey his commandments.

"2. Therefore, after justification, do as many good works as you can; but build not your rest and peace of mind upon them; for our best works are very imperfect and impure, and the sight of their imperfection banishes inward peace. Therefore build, and trust alone on the work of the Redeemer; then your peace will be founded on an immovable rock. Yet, constrained by love and gratitude, you must be exceedingly diligent in all good works: but when you have done all that is commanded, you must not esteem yourself, on that account, as righteous and holy, but as an unprofitable servant. For your ability to perform good works is owing to the grace of the Redeemer. Before he had forgiven your sins, and given you his righteousness, together with his mind and Spirit—in short, before justification—you could perform no truly good work whatever.

" 3. But to what degree, and how long must you bear your misery and distress? Only, (1,) till all that is sinful and vain is offensive to you ; (2,) till you despair of all human aid, and of your ability to help yourself ; and lastly, (3,) till you throw yourself at the feet of Jesus in prayer, and lay hold of his righteousness as your only refuge. The sooner you come to Jesus, the sooner will your distress cease."

Among the Roman Catholics in Wiggensbach and its neighbourhood were many persons, who, failing to find comfort, either by attending the confessional, or by receiving absolution from the priests, retired into convents, where they hoped to obtain relief for their spiritual wants. Of this class was a female, who, having been disgusted with the world, formed the design of entering a nunnery, or, at least, a clergyman's family, imagining that, in such a retreat, she would lead a holy and happy life. Accordingly, she withdrew to a nunnery, with a feeling of ecstacy, as if entering heaven itself.

But she found there no spiritual life—no Saint Theresa—and told her associates that they were no nuns, but mere hood-wearers. She soon left them, and then tried what pilgrimages could do for her. She travelled twice to Maria Einsiedel, in Switzerland, but the second time came back more uneasy and dissatisfied than before. She intreated her parish priest to tell her some other method of appeasing the inexpressible longings of her heart; but to no purpose. He only taxed her with pride and folly, and asked her whether she was not learned enough, or whether she wanted to be wiser than himself. At last she consulted Boos, and found what her soul had been seeking; he led her to Jesus, and in him she found the rest and comfort which he offers to the weary and heavy laden. From that time she felt no delight in her rosary, and other formal devotions. This disturbed her, and she almost suspected herself of heresy. She laid the matter before Boos. He asked her what so occupied her time and thoughts, that she could no longer use her rosary. "I do nothing, and think of nothing," she replied, "but to love Jesus, because he is in me, and with me." "You can do nothing better than that," said Boos; "it is no heresy to love Jesus, and think of him. To do everything out of love to him, is of more worth than using many rosaries." This satisfied her for awhile; but soon after, the thought struck her, " This clergyman makes so little account of rosaries, perhaps he is not of much worth himself." She went and told him, with fear and trembling, what had passed through her mind. Boos laughed heartily, and said, " Yes, you are in the right; in myself I am of no worth, but what I have taught you is of worth, for it was taught by Jesus Christ and his apostles; that remains true: continue, then, in the faith; do good, and shun evil."

Not long after, a feast of indulgences was held in her neighbourhood; but, instead of attending it, she went to Boos, fifteen miles off. On his asking her the reason, she said, " Jesus is my absolution, since he died for me. His blood, simply and alone, is the absolution for all my sins." " But who teaches you this?" said Boos. " No one," she replied; " the thought comes of itself into my mind, Jesus takes away my sins, and those things, too, on which I have depended so much, but have found them to afford neither rest nor peace. I am now convinced that all is of no avail, unless Jesus takes away sin, and dwells in our hearts." Boos then gave her a New Testament. She frequently visited him, and brought others to him for spiritual advice; amongst others, the curate of her own village.

CHAPTER IV.

Effects of his preaching—Persecution of his converts, and
of himself.

THE success which attended the labours of
Boos struck all who witnessed it with astonishment. They were at a loss to account for that
"faith working by love," that meekness and
humility, which were so conspicuous in his
converts. Their surprise was soon exchanged
for hatred, and they actually accused these
pious people of having intercourse with the
devil.

A father, for instance, who had been previously full of affection for his daughter, could
no longer endure her after she became a
Christian. His animosity seemed to increase
in proportion to her humility, gentleness, and
filial obedience. "You only put on that
sanctimonious manner," he exclaimed, "in
order to cloak your devilry. Away! you are
nothing but a hypocrite!" At last, in the heat
of passion, he drove her from his house. The
poor girl at first shed a torrent of tears. But
she soon recovered her composure, and her
spirits were revived by calling to mind the

Saviour's words which she had read a few days
before : " They shall expel you from their
synagogues, and persecute you from city to
city." She even rejoiced in suffering for the
sake of Jesus. (When Boos heard of it, he
said, " As the sea casts out its dead, so does
the world that which is dead to it.") She
prayed for her father ; and God graciously
heard her request. In a few days, he followed
her to a town at some distance, fell at her feet,
begged her to forgive him for his cruel treatment, and acknowledged that it was not her,
but himself, whom the devil had seduced.

A priest one day visited a sick person who
had been converted by the ministry of Boos,
and talked entirely on different subjects. After
he had left, the nurse, a pious woman, exclaimed, " What kind of clergyman is that ?
he said not one word about religion !" " Alas !"
said the invalid, " it is just the same in his
sermons ; he almost recommends dancing from
the pulpit." When he called again, the nurse
asked him why he said nothing about Christ.
He replied, with a smile, " Oh ! I cannot tell
what kind of a person he is, till I am dead !"
Shocked at his levity and ignorance, the good
woman prayed in silence for him, " Blessed
Jesus ! behold how blind he is ; give him
something of what thou hast given me, since
thou hast dwelt in my heart." She then
repeated several passages of the New Testament
to him, and offered to write them down, but he
seemed perfectly unmoved, and went away.

However, she did as she had purposed, and at his next visit gave him several passages of Scripture written out, and still continued·to pray for him. At night, out of mere curiosity, he read the texts, and was so much affected by them, that he wept bitterly. One text which peculiarly struck him was 2 Cor. xiii. 5, " Examine yourselves, whether ye be in the faith ; prove your own selves. Know ye not your own selves, how that Jesus Christ is in you, except ye be reprobates?" He then went to the nurse, who was ill herself, and told her the impressions he had received. He felt persuaded that the effect on his mind was owing to a Divine power, and expressed his gratitude both to God and herself. He also requested to be introduced to Boos, who was not a little agitated when he saw him coming, not being aware of the change that had taken place. On seeing and hearing him, he could scarcely believe his own senses. But so frank and unreserved was his confession, that Boos could not doubt his sincerity. He seemed ready, like Augustine, to lay open his heart to the whole world. From that time his exemplary conduct and zeal in preaching excited universal astonishment. As he often said, preaching the gospel was his life, and dying would be his gain.

On new year's day, 1797, Boos preached at Wiggensbach with extraordinary unction and energy. It was, says his biographer, as if he had poured forth streams of fire. But the effects were very different on different individuals. While many of his hearers were filled with joy, gratitude, and love, others were inflamed with anger, vexation, and hatred. The latter class demanded of the vicar the immediate dismissal of Boos, while the others entreated that he might remain. The uproar lasted all day, and throughout the night. By turns, each party gained the ascendency over the incumbent, a man of feeble and timid character, but who was kindly disposed towards Boos, having been his school-fellow. On this occasion, however, the fear of man prevailed. Instead of standing by his friend in the hour of trial, he yielded to the impetuous demands of misguided zeal, and dismissed the faithful witness of the truth.

This success of the enemies of the gospel was the signal for a general persecution at Kempten, and the places adjacent. The converts were dragged before the magistrates, and their houses ransacked. But when the magistrates found that no charge could be substantiated against them, excepting the ardour of their devotion, they dismissed them as silly pietists, but without promising them any protection. This lenity of their judges only stimulated the fury of the persecutors, who raised an outcry against them everywhere, in the pulpits, streets, and taverns. Some were obliged to remain in obscure retreats for five or six months. Others were tracked like wild beasts to their hiding-places, and forced to leave their kindred and native country for ever. The whole diocese of Kempten was a scene of the most violent agitation. And what was the crime of these victims of fanaticism? Simply that of receiving Jesus as their Saviour, and living according to the holy commandments of the word of God.

Meanwhile Boos had retired to a village, and shunned all notoriety. He even forbad persons to speak of him, but the reputation of his piety spread more widely every day. The hatred and envy of the priests rose proportionably higher. "He is a seducer and a heretic," they cried. "See how he draws the people after him! He wants to found a new sect, and overturn the Catholic religion." Every pulpit resounded with charges of heresy against the pacific Boos. Men who had never preached in favour of the truth, or at least only in a very lukewarm, unimpressive manner, now harangued loudly and incessantly against it. The very name of Boos was so odious, that no one could pronounce it in a friendly tone without the risk of being roughly handled. A man in the village of Wertach having spoken a word in his favour, received such a violent blow on his chest that he broke a blood-vessel, and died in a few days. Yet the person who committed this outrage was never called to account. Not a revengeful word escaped the lips of the poor sufferer; on his death-bed he forgave his murderer, and exhorted his wife to return good for evil.

CHAPTER V.

AT the instigation of certain priests, the civil and ecclesiastical authorities cast into prison some of the most faithful friends of Boos, especially such of the clergy as were known to be attached to him.

The following may serve as a specimen of the interrogatories that were put to a priest who was accused of having imbibed the heresies of Boos.

Judge. Are you acquainted with the doctrines taught by Martin Boos?

Priest. Yes.

Judge. In what do they consist?

Priest. He teaches us repentance and faith in Jesus Christ.

Judge. What do you understand by believing in Jesus Christ?

Priest. When a man enlightened by the grace of God, is conscious of being a miserable sinner, he rejoices to believe in a Redeemer, and to receive pardon as a free gift. The Israelites who were bitten by the fiery serpent, had only to look on the brazen serpent which Moses had set up, and they were instantly cured; and thus the sinner, by looking to Christ, obtains a cure for his spiritual maladies, and the salvation of his soul.

Judge. By what sign do you know that Christ is in you?

Priest. St. John says, " Whosoever shall confess that Jesus is the Son of God, God dwelleth in him, and he in God." The tree is known by its fruits. Where Christ is there is peace, joy, patience, meekness, purity, and the hope of eternal salvation.

Judge. What is the difference between the disciples of John and those of Jesus?

Priest. The disciples of John are those who repent, and who are thus prepared to receive Christ. The disciples of Jesus are those who believe in him, and who by faith have received him into their hearts.

Judge. How did you arrive at this belief?

Priest. For a long time I had been tormented by my doubts and sins. Philosophy only aggravated the malady of my soul. I found no relief in the observance of the outward acts of religion. Some conversations which I had with a very respectable man, enlightened my mind a little. Certain pious clergymen gave me some texts of the Bible; I read them, and the sense of my sins revived in me in a way altogether new. I then paid a visit to Martin Bros at Wiggensbach. He exhibited Jesus to me as "the Lamb of God that taketh away the sins of the world," and spoke largely to me of the happiness which Jesus gives. I believed the gospel, and felt peace and joy in my heart, accompanied with an ardent desire to be converted to Christ.

Judge. Have you made use of no external ceremony?

Priest. No; of none whatever.

Judge. Do you expect any miracle?

Priest. No.

Judge. Do you believe that these doctrines are calculated to make men better?

Priest. Yes, without doubt. I have always had that opinion since I have known them.

Such was the evidence on which this pious clergyman was condemned to leave the country, and to seek for a new home.

But to return to Boos. He could not remain long in his quiet retreat, but was once more turned adrift without resources, employment, or shelter. He could not return among those whom he regarded as his spiritual children, for his doing so would have inevitably exposed them to cruel persecutions. He, therefore, requested Feneburg, with whom he had been curate three years before, to grant him an asylum. The vicar of Seeg rejoiced in the thought of having under his roof a man who had suffered so much for the gospel, and, as he was unable to leave home through lameness, sent one of his friends to meet him. This person, as soon as he caught sight of Boos mounted on an old grey horse,

cried out, " Whither are going, St. Martin, on
your grey horse? Peace be to thee!" Feneburg
received him with heartfelt joy, remembering
the words of Jesus, "He that receiveth you, receiveth me ; and he that receiveth me, receiveth
him that sent me."

This season of repose for Boos did not last
long. Scarcely a month had elapsed when an
ecclesiastical counsellor, named Rössle, made
his appearance at the vicarage of Seeg, apprehended Boos without showing any warrant,
broke open his desk, seized all his papers,
even the most confidential, and then made off
with his booty without waiting for Feneburg's
return, who had only left home for a few hours
on a visit to a neighbour.

This modern Saul (who, however, alas! never
became a Paul) would have taken Boos away
at the same time, had he not been too ill to be
removed; but he extorted a pledge from him
to make his appearance at the bishop's court, as
soon as his health would permit. Boos knew
that "bonds and imprisonment awaited him ;"
but having given his word, on the 10th of February, 1797, he presented himself before the
ecclesiastical tribunal at Augsburg.

The first step taken with Boos was to confine
him in the house of correction, at Goeggingen,
a league from the city, where none but crimi-
nals or lunatics of the clerical order were
admitted. From this place he was brought to
be examined at Augsburg, in the custody of a
soldier, as if he had been some notorious culprit.

He was kept in imprisonment for eight months, during which he underwent more than fifty examinations. At his earnest request, he was allowed writing materials, but all correspondence with his friends or other persons was strictly forbidden. Yet it beguiled the tedious hours of his captivity to commit his meditations to writing, to retrace all the goodness of the Lord to him, and to record the reasons for the hope that was in him.

The following extracts from his journal will exhibit the state of his mind at this period.

"I should have fallen into the depths of despair, O my God, at the sight of my innumerable sins, if thy word had not enlightened my steps. This celestial light dispelled my doubts, and caused my heart to glow with the liveliest hope. When we were enemies then thou gavest us thy Son, our heavenly Advocate. In his precious blood is all my confidence. It is in reliance on him, and not on my works, that I aspire to the full enjoyment of thy glorious presence. Christ *for* us—Christ *in* us; here is the basis of our salvation and sanctification; here is the source of every good work. But how many persons are there who would fain raise the edifice of their virtues on another foundation! Their building will soon sink in ruins."

"In our day, as formerly, Christ is rejected, maltreated, dragged before unjust judges, and condemned to an infamous death."

"There is a communion of saints, which

becomes more and more intimate through the medium of Christian love.

" There are on earth only two churches, the true and the false. How few belong to the first! Among the best Catholics, and in the Protestant church, there are a multitude of Judaizers, that is, men who trust in their own righteousness, and who will not submit to the true righteousness which comes from God alone."

" Good works cannot procure our pardon, but it is impossible to be saved without them. Some good fruits necessarily proceed from a good tree; and the righteousness of God received by us, is a fountain which pours itself forth into a thousand streams of good works. When men begin to become better, they commonly go from the hope of reward, or the dread of punishment, to the law school of Moses, then to the repentance school of John, next to the cross school of Jesus, and lastly to the school of the Holy Ghost."

" In preaching Moses and the law, you are far less exposed to persecution than in preaching Christ and his gospel. Why is this? Because people are much more Jewish than Christian, and Satan is less roused to opposition if men are not shown the means and the power by which they can obey God's commands."

" The law only tells men what they ought to do ; but Christ gives the disposition and the ability to do it. It is, therefore, only doing our work by halves, if we only preach the law to people, and say nothing of the power to fulfil it, obtained through Christ."

" Judaism and heathenism have so gained the ascendency in Christendom that the preachers of the pure gospel are treated as the apostles were—they are ' everywhere spoken against.' "

" The mere law points out the will of God, which is to be fulfilled ; and shows what sin is; but it gives no power to obey the former, or to avoid and procure pardon for the latter. Our preachers, for fear of becoming Lutheran, preach the law too much, and living faith in *Christ for us and in us*, too little."

The governor of the house of correction at Goeggingen was an ecclesiastic, named Hoffmann. Accustomed to see in the persons placed under his inspection none but evil-doers, who deserved the utmost severity of the law, he regarded Boos, when he was brought in, as a criminal and a vile heretic. He was greatly astonished to behold the humility, gentleness, patience, and piety of his new prisoner. He could scarcely believe his eyes. At first he thought that such a pious exterior must proceed from hypocrisy ; but his conversations with Boos entirely removed the misapprehension. Boos related so frankly the events of his past life, and explained his religious principles with such simplicity and clearness, that the governor was deeply affected, and said to himself, " This is Divine ! this is indeed extraordinary! None of us possess it! Oh that I were so!"

"And so you can be," replied Boos, "and I wish all the world were so, except these bonds. Only believe in Jesus Christ; believe that he can deliver you from the prison of sin and unbelief; believe that he can and will give you release from the bondage of sin; and the thing is done."

The Lord blessed these words of his servant. Hoffmann believed, and from that time was of one heart and one soul with his prisoner, who felt the rigour of his confinement alleviated, and his faith strengthened, by this happy result.

Meanwhile, the process against Boos was going on. He was brought many times before the ecclesiastical court at Augsburg. He calmly replied to all the questions that were put to him, and proved that the doctrines he taught were founded on the Bible, and in accordance with the Fathers and the Liturgy of the church. His judges, in violation of the impartiality that belonged to their office, exerted their utmost ingenuity to substantiate the charges against him; and searched for heresies and crimes where it was impossible to find any. They cited before them Feneburg and his curate, and thirty-seven other persons, who were accused of being partizans of Boos. The first two were subjected to solitary confinement for a week in the convent, and obliged to perform acts of penance and contrition. Several priests, actuated by a blind and diabolical zeal, wrote to Nigg, the vicar-general, and urged him to burn one of the heretics as an example. The vicar-general was favourable to Boos and his friends, but wanted energy and boldness to plead their cause. However, to shorten the investigation, he destroyed several packets of letters and other manuscripts, which might have been employed to criminate Boos.

After Boos had been detained eight months, he was at last sentenced to be kept as a prisoner within the city walls, and to be suspended for a year from every ecclesiastical function, in order that he might give himself afresh to the study of theology, and learn to correct his errors.

The impression made on his mind by these trying events will be best understood by his own description, in a letter to a friend, dated September 22, 1797.

" I am glad that you have not been too much irritated at my condemnation. But, after all, there was something strange about it. Two months ago, my *Adam* protested violently in secret against this cup, and almost sweat drops of blood ; but I laid him, ten times a day, as a whole burnt-offering on the altar, and gave myself to the Lord. By so doing I set my mind at rest, and could look forward to my condemnation with joy, and hoped I should continue in the same state of mind. But when the governor, a fortnight before the sentence was passed, told me it would be a twelvemonths' imprisonment, *Adam* could not endure the thought of being sacrificed, but struggled might and main against it. I bound him again hand and foot, and laid him on the altar, so that he was obliged to submit. But on the 10th of September my sister came to the prison, and told me that I should be sentenced to the house of correction for a year. Oh what a blow was that! And that *she* should be the person to tell me of it, pierced me to the heart.

"The next morning, at four o'clock, I went from Bethany (Goeggingen) to Jerusalem (Augsburg), thinking, 'To-day thou wilt be solemnly condemned in the presence of thy fathers and brethren.' I prayed, and rejoiced, and wept, by turns, and waited in the grove till the gates were opened. I then went to Siller's cell, and poured forth the anguish of my heart; he comforted and strengthened me like an angel. At nine o'clock I stood on Golgotha. I was the first; the other brethren followed, but we could not converse before so many Malchuses. We were now summoned... I placed myself last. There sat the seven ecclesiastical councillors, and here stood the four culprits. In the middle was placed a crucifix, a praying-desk covered with red cloth, with an open missal upon it. The vicar-general took out a sheet of paper, called upon me to step forwards into the middle of the room, and then, with angry looks and in a very loud tone, read my sentence of a year's imprisonment in the house of correction. While this was going on, I felt a heavenly calm, as if it concerned me not. But when the vicar had finished, my *Adam* groaned, and I said, I submit to this sentence because I consider it as God's appointment. But it is dreadfully severe. I had hoped that on this day my punishment would have come to an end, whereas it is, strictly speaking, only beginning. I was then ordered to kneel at the praying-desk, and repeat aloud my confession of faith ; the other brethren knelt behind me on the ground. Feneburg stood leaning on his stick.

" The vicar next handed me ten propositions on fine paper, tied with a gold thread. I had never seen them before. I was required to abjure them. At first I refused, and asked why they had not been previously submitted to my consideration, for I wished clearly to understand what I was so solemnly to recant, I read each proposition twice, and remarked upon each what was given me to say at the moment. I sighed aloud, and showed how deeply I felt the gross misrepresentation of my sentiments and conduct. No attention was paid to my protest or explanations. The brethren were then called up, and at last we were all dismissed."

When Boos was released from his prison-house, he was still not allowed to go beyond the city walls. He hired a small apartment, poorly furnished, and had his dinner brought to him in an earthen vessel, called a triangle, such as poor students and beggars are wont to use. In order to comply with that part of his sentence which imposed upon him the renewed study of theology, he applied to father Ulrich, the dean of the Capuchin monastery, who had himself been persecuted in his youth. He was a venerable old man, of enlightened piety, and well known as the author of several religious works.

During Boos's detention at Augsburg, he made a very gratifying discovery. One day, while turning over the volumes at a second-hand book-stall, finding some religious books with which he was not acquainted, he asked the dealer, "What sort of books are these?" The man replied, "They are such as our saints use." "Saints!" said Boos; "of what sort?" "They are people who do nothing but pray and sing psalms," was the answer: "they keep aloof from the world. They are singular people, who profess to be better than their neighbours. For my part, I have no great opinion of them; I suspect they are hypocrites; we must do like the rest of the world."

"This is strange," thought Boos; "there is something behind which I must find out. What the world vilifies and rejects is certainly not of the world, for the world would love its own. I must make further inquiries." He asked, therefore, where these *saints* lived. The bookseller readily informed him; and Boos had the pleasure of finding at least fifty persons in Augsburg who rejoiced in Christ Jesus as their hope for time and eternity, and who, on that account, were, like himself, despised and persecuted by an ungodly world. They told him, also, of a great number of others who were animated with the same faith.

A young student, who was also a private teacher in Augsburg, was in the habit of hearing Boos and his friends spoken of in very opprobrious terms. But several things which were imputed to them as heretical or criminal, appeared to him commendable. The consequence was, he was anxious to become acquainted with an individual who was so much spoken against, and at last obtained an interview with Boos.

Staublein (that was the student's name) found Boos a very different man from what he had been represented to be. He visited him frequently, and by degrees the truth made a lodgment in his heart. A student, like every one who is devoted almost exclusively to intellectual pursuits, often requires a much longer time to understand the doctrines of Christ, and to submit himself to the obedience of faith, than the simple-hearted artisan. At length, like St. Paul, he could say, "Lord, what wilt thou have me to do?" Possessing considerable abilities, and a teachable disposition, he appeared to be fitted for much usefulness. His health, however, declined, and he was obliged to relinquish his studies, and return to his native place in the country, where he continued to labour, as far as his strength would permit, for two years, when he finished his earthly course.

CHAPTER VI.

Unexpected liberation—Settlement at Langeneifnach—Again
summoned before the Ecclesiastical Court.

Boos, to his great surprise, was set at liberty
in January, 1798, after eight months' imprisonment, and four months' detention within the
city walls. He was very much indebted on
this occasion to the good offices of father Ulric,
with whom he had been *repeating* his theological studies. This venerable man declared
that Boos was a better theologian than himself,
and warmly pleaded his cause with his judges.
In consequence, he not only regained his
personal liberty, but was permitted to resume
the pastoral functions. The appointment he
received was at Langeneifnach, about seven
leagues from Augsburg; the vicar of the parish
was Koch, formerly governor of the ecclesiastical house of correction at Goeggingen.

On being settled in his new charge, he wrote
to his friends at Augsburg as follows :—" By
the grace of God, I am perfectly well. I
preached again for the first time here on
February 18. The Lord prospered his word,
as spoken by me. Both I and the congregation

were deeply moved. There seem to be some well-disposed persons here who are in earnest about salvation. . . . But we shall be brought back to Jerusalem to pay for the wine we have drunk in communion with one another ; (that is, we shall be persecuted for that spiritual joy which we have had in communion with the Lord.) . . . Well, if it cannot be otherwise, if we must endure suffering and martyrdom, we will not hesitate to return. My reason for saying this is, that, like a burnt child, I dread the fire, and my superior has received orders to keep a watchful eye over all my words and actions, and especially my correspondence ; which he has already shown his readiness to do. But this shall not alter my determination to preach the doctrine of the cross. Only pray that we may joyfully suffer the reproach of Christ, and not draw back, but crucify our earthly and sensual desires, since flesh and blood cannot inherit the kingdom of God."

In another letter to his friend Staublein, he writes :— " I rejoice to believe that the holy Scripture comforts you as it does myself. I am quite convinced that, in order to become what we ought to be, we require three schools. First, the *repentance-school* of John the Baptist, which baptizes with water, and purifies from gross and outward sin. Secondly, the *cross-school* of Jesus, which mocks, scourges, crucifies, kills, and buries our Adam, whether gross or refined. Thirdly, the *fire-school* of the Holy Ghost, which baptizes with fire and love, seizing and consuming our most subtle corruptions. Whoever has studied in these schools, let him come and be our teacher. Whoever is ignorant of them, let him keep at a distance from us, and go where he pleases. The Bible informs us respecting these three schools. God grant us his Holy Spirit as an interpreter !

"The brethren at S. would have written to you long ago, but they were afraid of those about you. Tell them not to tremble ; it is the weakness of their faith. We must go again to Jerusalem, (so they call Augsburg since the Christian high court is there, which crucifies Christ, as formerly at Jerusalem ;) there is no exemption for the disciples of Jesus. An untried faith may be no faith ; any one may have a faith of the fancy or of the lips ; it is, therefore, worthless. You have found the truth of my favourite saying—' Among children we may meet with men, but among men with no children.' Truly the Father will have us to be children, or we cannot enter the kingdom of heaven, but we must be content to become fools in the eyes of the world.

"Do not think it hard if you are not always enjoying the light, but are occasionally in darkness and sorrow. It is thus with myself ; and it must be so. The salt of the sufferings of Jesus must be mingled with our whole life. And you must not attempt to free yourself by force from the pressure of your trials, but wait till He comes, who will shed light on

what by nature is cold and dark. Many
thousands followed Jesus, and rejoiced in his
light, but when the hour of darkness came,
they forsook him. Surely you will not act
thus ? May the grace of Jesus be with you !"

Boos had scarcely enjoyed a short season of
repose for about two months at Langeneifnach,
and begun to see some fruits of his labours,
when his adversaries once more took the field
against him. The abbot of Kempten, and the
other prelates and deans in the country, protested loudly against his release, and demanded
that he should be imprisoned for the rest of
his days. They endeavoured to justify this
iniquitous severity on the ground of an intercepted letter from Boos to one of his persecuted
fellow-Christians. In their prejudiced eyes,
the mere expressions of sympathy with his
brethren, constituted a crime. Accordingly,
he was summoned to leave Langeneifnach, and
repair to Augsburg. He reached that city
April 3, 1798. But hesitating whether to
appear before his judges or to take to flight,
he consulted the friend with whom he lodged,
who gave his opinion in the words of our Lord,
" If they persecute you in one city, flee ye to
another." In accordance with this advice, he
took refuge with pastor Winkelhofer, at Munich,
who concealed him for three weeks in his own
chamber. He then removed from one place
to another, as no one dared to harbour him
long ; but wherever he went he disseminated

the gospel, reminding those who had received it that "through much tribulation we must enter the kingdom of God." He was often reduced to great straits. At last, partly from necessity, and partly from a sense of his own incompetence for the clerical office, he thought of engaging himself as a herdsman at a farmer's. Something, however, in his manner betrayed his real station, and the master of the house immediately saluted him with great respect as a clergyman. Boos remained with him long enough to instruct him in the way of salvation, and had the satisfaction of leading him to a living faith in Christ. But, wearied with this uncertain mode of life, he returned, on the 1st of July, to pastor Winkelhofer, and on the 4th he went to Sailer, who, in order to find a retreat for him, wrote to an old friend, Benedict Scharl, steward of the estate of Groenbach, not far from Hohenlinde, in Bavaria, the following laconic epistle :—

"Scharl ! come with a carriage and horses, and fetch a friend whom I recommend to you. Take him into your house and heart, without asking who or what he is, and treat him as you would myself."

The worthy man did as he was requested, and took Sailer's unknown friend, whom he called Zobo (an anagram of Boos or Booz,) without asking him a single question. It so happened, however, that a few months after, a clergyman who had known Boos in former years called at the house, and on seeing him,

exclaimed, " Boos! what brought you here?"
His incognito was thus at an end ; but the
only alteration it made in the conduct of his
host was, that he treated him, if possible,
with more affection and respect than before,
especially after Boos had told him his whole
history. The only reason for concealing his
name from Scharl was, that if he had been
asked respecting Boos, he might say that he
knew no person of that name.

The enemies of Boos at last found out his
hiding-place ; and on December 9, 1798, he
was forced to leave his kind host, and betake
himself once more to Augsburg. " Weary of
inaction and concealment," he writes, " I threw
myself again into the hands of my enemies at
Augsburg, saying, Here I am, tear me in
pieces, if you will ! They were astonished at
my coming ; their reception and treatment of
me were more gentle than I expected."

Boos was summoned before his judges four
times in the course of December, and ques-
tioned minutely respecting the friends with
whom he had resided or carried on correspondence ; but he would make no disclosures
to the injury of persons to whom he was indebted for his liberty and life. On being asked
why he had fled, he answered in the words of
the man who was born blind, (John ix. 27,)
" I have told you already, and ye did not hear:
wherefore would ye hear it again?" This
reply so irritated the fiscal that he quite lost
his self-command, and abruptly closed the

examination. Boos passed the winter at Augsburg, in his own hired house, under the protection of the vicar-general, though for four months he was not allowed to go beyond the city walls.

The vicar-general held Boos in high esteem ; and often slipped · a louis d'or into his hand with an express injunction to say nothing about it. He would gladly have set him entirely at liberty had that been possible. But seeing that there was no probability of his remaining unmolested in that part of the country, he advised him to remove to a distance. Boos adopted his advice, and left Augsburg on the 29th of April, 1799, in company with another persecuted and expelled clergyman ; and being furnished with a recommendatory letter from a devoted friend, proceeded in a vessel down the Lech and the Danube to Austria, and entered the diocese of Lintz, of which Joseph Anthony Gall was the bishop.

CHAPTER VII.

Boos in Austria—Extracts from his Journal.

The bishop of Lintz gave Boos a very kind reception. After becoming acquainted with him, he often exclaimed, " Oh that they would send me twenty such priests as Boos!" He gave him a temporary appointment at Leonding, near Lintz, preparatory to his being settled at Waldneukirch. Here, by his energetic preaching, his attention to the sick and to all in distress, and the exemplary purity of his conduct, he soon acquired the esteem and confidence both of his ecclesiastical superiors and his parishioners. At the end of two years he became assistant to professor Bertgen, at Peuerbach, and remained five years in that parish. The following letter from an Austrian clergyman, with some extracts from his own journal, will give sufficient information respecting his labours during that period.

" Martin," says this clergyman, " was my nearest neighbour for several years at Peuerbach. We often met, and the frank disclosures he made of his inward state, impressed me with the purity of his character. He was unwearied in his pastoral duties. He was diligent not only in his labours out of doors, such as visiting the sick, catechising, and inspecting, but also in his study. He committed to paper at the beginning of the week all his addresses for the school or the pulpit. Frequently have I called on him on a Monday or Tuesday, and found that he had already written his sermon for the following Sunday. He was uncommonly rich in striking thoughts, allusions, and expressions. I never heard him preach, as our services were held at the same hour ; but, from the effects produced by his discourses, it may be concluded that they were full of spirit and life.

"In corresponding and communicating information, or making remarks, and that fully, kindly, promptly, and punctually, he was an incomparable friend : his beautiful, delicate hand-writing was seasoned with zeal, and peace, and living Christianity. His thoughts, recollections, and views were always full of scriptural allusions, which were constantly at his command.

"The abundance of his mental resources, and his unwearied activity, enabled him to perform so much within so short a time. Very early in the morning, and late at night, he was seated at his desk ; and before the bell called him to the daily service, he had written several letters, or other documents."

EXTRACTS FROM BOOS' JOURNAL, 1803.

July 6.—" If the emperor were to send a
message by his son, saying, ' My good people,
take no thought for your life, what ye shall
eat, or how ye shall be clothed, for my father
knoweth what ye need ; he has an abundance
of such things with which to supply all your
need ; only make it your concern to do his
will, and obey the laws of his kingdom :'—on
receiving such a message, all would rejoice and
feel at ease. Yet God has long ago sent
exactly such a message by his Son ; but how
few persons rejoice in it, and have their
anxieties laid to rest by it ! A sign that men
put less trust in God than in the emperor !"

July 7.—" ' Stir up the gift that is in thee,'
says Paul to Timothy. It seems as if grace,
light, zeal, and courage, sometimes sleep in us,
since Paul exhorts us to stir up or awaken
them. At least it is so with myself. Often it
seems as if all light were extinguished, all
zeal cooled down, all courage gone. This state
often lasts two or three days. All at once,
there is a revival, as if all these things had
been sleeping, and now awoke from their
slumbers."

July 9.—" It is an excellent remark of professor Sailer's, that a man may study away his
understanding. Most men of learning are unfit for the world, for they have another unreal
world in their heads, and therefore know not

how to use the one before them. This is simply because they are always poring over their books, and never look into the world, particularly the one within them, that is, their own hearts.

July 11.—"Those persons are more pleasing to God who wish to receive something from him, than those who would come to him with a present. The Pharisee was in his own eyes rich in good works, and wished to present some of them to God; but he says, I want nothing from thee! But the publican came destitute, and besought of God grace, pardon, and justification; and God gave him what he desired and needed. The poor are filled with good things, while the rich are sent empty away."

July 12.—"It seems to me as if God acted towards men in a progressively kind and condescending manner. Under the old dispensation punishments were inflicted for comparatively minor transgressions. Under the new dispensation, God's strokes are fewer, slower, often withheld altogether. In the former dispensation God made himself known to men only as Jehovah, as that Being who is, and was, and will be, as the God of Abraham, Isaac, and Jacob. In the latter, he allows himself to be called Father, Son, Brother, Holy Ghost, Comforter. All this is far more kind and condescending."

July 15.—"A person once said to me, 'I have something on my mind that I dare not tell to any one, not even to you, and yet it often weighs me down.' 'Tell it to God,' said I, 'for we may tell him everything, good and bad, little and great; yes, everything.' Whereupon she told me what troubled her."

July 16.—"The Pharisees could not give the Saviour any proper answer to the question, 'What think ye of Christ? whose Son is he?' though they were constantly hearing and reading of him. What they were destitute of, was the most excellent knowledge of Christ. (Phil. iii. 8.) So it is with many Christians in the present day; they hear and read much of Christ; every week they speak of his sufferings and death; and yet only a few can give any right account of him. Had they the most excellent knowledge of Christ, they would, with Paul, count everything else as dung; but since other things please them more than Christ, they have not the right knowledge of him."

July 18.—"Some persons, when in mental or bodily suffering, make a pilgrimage to a shrine of the virgin Mary, or some other saint. To such I cannot help saying, 'My friends, what think ye of Christ? whose Son is he?' Your pilgrimages show that as yet you know him not, for you put more trust in his mother and the saints than in him. But did his mother ever say, 'Come unto me, and I will give you rest?' Did she not rather say, 'Whatsoever he saith unto you, do?'"

July 19.—"When a scholar or a theologian is proud of his theological attainments, he makes it evident that he does not yet know Christ. For if he knew Christ he would also know that without leaning on Christ he could neither go, nor stand, nor do, nor think, nor desire anything good; and, consequently, all pride would leave him."

July 22.—" Christ in the heart, and a cross on the shoulders: this is the badge of all true Christians."

July 24.—"'The consequences of sin are often slow, but sure. The rich man fared sumptuously every day, till the day when he lifted up his eyes in hell being in torment. 'For twenty years I have been used to get drunk,' said a sot, when his health failed him, 'and yet I have never been the worse for it till now.'"

July 27.—Boos said to some women who were complaining that they had such profligate husbands, who did nothing but gamble and drink, "Good folks, all this talking and grumbling does neither you nor your husbands any good. Rather take your husbands, as his friends took the paralytic mentioned in the gospel, to the Saviour by prayer; and when Jesus sees your faith and tears he will be at last constrained to say, 'Be of good cheer, daughter, I will help thee, and convert thy husband.'"

July 28.—" As I have a weak and delicate stomach, the richest food is exactly that which is least suited for me ; it only makes my stomach weaker. And because I have a heart not sufficiently grounded in humility, great honours, titles, and offices, are not good for me."

August 4.—"Avarice takes money both from the friends and the enemies of God. Elisha's servant took it from the former; Judas from the latter."

August 5.—" Beware of falling; for not all who fall rise again. Peter rose ; but Judas remained fallen, or rather fell deeper."

August 27.—" 'What will my boon companions say if I no longer gamble and drink with them as heretofore?' said a young man whom I was exhorting to alter his way of life. I replied, When such men ridicule your altered way of life, it is just the same as if people who have a wen on their necks were to ridicule those who have not. But if the good opinion of your boon companions is dearer to you than being honoured by God and his holy angels, it is all over with you; you will never be saved."

October 1.—" It is very sweet to love one's enemies and persecutors, and to do them good. I have attempted it again to-day. Here also is verified our Saviour's declaration, ' My yoke is easy, and my burden is light.' Men deny themselves much happiness when they neglect to do what Jesus commanded, and did. Whoever will know whether his doctrine be of God, let him do it."

October 10.—" There are some who look upon it as a weakness, to forgive a person who insults them. By this rule, God would be the weakest being in heaven or earth, since no one forgives so much as he does."

October 18.—" Death strips us of the glory

with which the world has attired us, just as a boot-jack draws off our boots. Another person wears my boots when I am dead, and another takes my glory. Of how little value is it then!"

October 22.—"Even in Paradise, the three-fold lust mentioned by John showed and developed itself. 1. The lust of the flesh, in longing to eat the fruit. 2. The lust of the eye, in being pleased with the sight of it; and, 3. The pride of life, in the desire after knowledge and earthly elevation."

October 23.—"What was man's clothing, before he sinned? Answer. The robe of innocence.

"Who gave it him? God himself.

"Who took it from him? The devil and sin.

"Who restores it to him? Christ."

May 1, 1804.—"The man who is to be a good theologian, priest, bishop, or pastor, must previously, like Abraham, Joseph, Moses, and even the Lord Jesus, have passed through trials of all kinds, and have been preserved. The devil must have sifted him like wheat, without his falling through or over the sieve."

May 3.—"If the preacher have not the hearts of his hearers in his hand, let him preach as well as he may, their heads will find fault with this or the other point. Those whose hearts Jesus possessed, said not, 'This is a hard saying, who can hear it?' but, 'To whom shall we go? thou hast the words of eternal life.'"

May 4.—"A candle is placed on a candle-stick, that people may see, and be benefited

by it. A teacher or preacher is placed in a
pulpit, that people may see and hear him, and
be benefited.   Now, when a man in this position is unholy or without spirit, without head
and heart, it is a monstrous absurdity."

May 5.—"A learned man without humility
will learn nothing from a common man.   The
very learned and extremely pious Pharisee
would not be taught by Jesus the carpenter;
hence true wisdom was hidden from him."

June 10.—" To see God and enjoy him in
love, will be our heaven in heaven.   But previously to serve him here, to assist in extend-
ing his kingdom, is, or at least might be, our
heaven upon earth; or a ladder by which we
might ascend to heaven.   O God, help me up
this ladder!"

June 20.—" When a field that is tolerably
good is left fallow for some years, it becomes
still better : so when a good and able man
is set aside, and, as it were, left fallow, he
thereby becomes still better and more useful;
at least, all things work together for good to
him that loves God; and so, lying fallow is for
his advantage."

July 14.—"Abraham offered to God what
was dearest to him.   Whoever does that now,
is an Abraham."

CHAPTER VIII.

Boos at Gallneukirch.

Boos was not permitted to remain long in obscurity. He was soon appointed minister at Postlingburg, a place not far from Lintz ; and in 1806, removed to a much larger parish, that of Gallneukirch. For four years and a half he laboured there without interruption or persecution. But as this calm was accompanied with little success in his ministry, it gave him little satisfaction. The seed was sown, but it produced no fruit. His grief on this account led him to redouble his efforts and his prayers. The melancholy end of one of his parishioners about this time, who, after leading a worldly and irreligious life, died in despair, also stimulated him to a still more earnest and faithful exhibition of the gospel.

Many of his parishioners suffered deeply from a sense of their sins. All their efforts, prayers, and confessions, failed to relieve their burdened consciences. They stood in continual fear of death and judgment. "The most devout among them," said Boos, "were conscious

of not having fulfilled that great *all* written
and prescribed in the law, and were ignorant
that 'the just must live by faith.' They
sought for salvation not in Christ crucified, but
in miserable expedients by which they attempted to cover their sins, and in good works,
which never gave them peace. The worse
portion of my parish lived at ease in sin, far
from Christ, without faith, hope, and love, as
well as without virtue. Such was the diseased
state of my flock. They might be divided into
two classes—Jewish Christians, and Pagan
Christians, with a sprinkling of true disciples
of Christ; and yet there were as many altogether as four or five thousand souls. Knowing
by my own experience, that there is no peace
nor true consolation for afflicted consciences,
but by means of a living faith in a crucified
Saviour, I insisted on the necessity of seeking
salvation and justification, not by the law or
by works, but by faith in Christ.

" The following were the principal points
which on different occasions I made the subject of my discourses: That all men are sinners
—that there is none righteous, no, not one
(Rom. iii. 10—18)—that no man can justify
himself, or make himself free from sin, and
capable of a new life; no man can merit
righteousness by praying, fasting, giving alms,
confessing, making pilgrimages, etc.; in short,
that pious works do not make a righteous and
pious man; but the pious and justified man
performs pious and good works.

" We are justified and saved, not by our own works, but by faith in the Son of God. His death is the procuring cause of our forgiveness. Only God is righteous, and he whom he makes righteous.

" Though good works do not justify and save us, they are not to be neglected ; for, 1, God requires and enjoins them ; 2, We prove, by means of them, our justification in the sight of God and man ; 3, They are necessary fruits and consequences of a living faith that works by love.

" Faith is a hearty, living confidence, and firm trust in the grace of God promised in Christ, for the forgiveness of sins and eternal life, kindled by the word of God, and the Holy Spirit.

" The forgiveness of sins is entirely gratuitous, without any merit of our own, of God's pure mercy for the merits of Christ. And this forgiveness of sins is the righteousness that avails us before God.

" When a person, alarmed on account of his sins, asks me what he must do to obtain peace and salvation, I do not, first of all, say, You must live piously, obey God's commands, and do good works ; but I say, first of all, Believe on Jesus Christ, who by his sacrifice on the cross has purchased for you the forgiveness of sins, the righteousness that avails before God, and eternal life ; and then, when, like the jailor at Philippi, a man is justified and set at rest by this faith I would say, ' Now live

holily; keep God's commandments out of
love to Him who by his death on the cross
justified thee, freed thee from sin and punishment, and made thee an heir of eternal life,
and capable of performing righteous works.
First make the tree good, says Christ, then will
the fruit be good. But I do not deny that
temporal punishments and chastisements may
still be sent by God; for he says, 'As many
as I love, I rebuke and chasten.'

"A Christian ought to live Christianly and
piously, and obey God's commands with the
utmost diligence; but never imagine that he
can thereby become righteous and holy before
God. We are indebted for true holiness and
righteousness, not to our own doing, and
suffering, but to the work and sufferings of
Christ.

"I would not wish to be in heaven, if every
one could merit it by his good works, and we
did not all find admittance there by grace.
For then, each one would be comparing his
own doing and suffering with that of others,
and there would be pride, envy, contention,
and jealousy in heaven, as there is on earth.
But if Christ alone has merited heaven for all,
and all who enter heaven are indebted to grace,
we may hope for peace and rest.

"True and living faith is not to be learned
from one's mother, or schoolmaster, or minister,
nor in seminaries or universities; but only in
the school of the Holy Spirit, after much
prayer, conflict, and humiliation of all kinds.

Still, useful institutions for instruction are not on that account to be rejected, but to be highly esteemed.

"All sacraments received without faith (by adults) are of little or no use. 'If thou believest with all thy heart, thou mayest,' said Philip to the eunuch, (Acts viii. 37.)

"Every Christian needs daily repentance, since he daily sins, not indeed by committing gross sins, but by falling short of that cheerful and perfect obedience which the spirit of the law requires.

"The law, it is true, does not justify, but it is, and ever will be, a sacred rule—the standard of our lives and of our filial obedience. It is also a clear mirror, which exhibits to us our sinful defilement. Christ has redeemed us from the *curse* of the law, but not from obedience to it. It is binding on a man as long as he lives.

"The language in James ii. 24, does not contradict that in the Epistle to the Romans. The former speaks of justification before men, the latter of justification before God. God alone can read our hearts; and as nothing is more deceitful than a mere confession of the lips, our justification must be evidenced by its fruits. Abraham was justified before God without the works of the law; but he was also to be acknowledged as just by men."

CHAPTER IX.

Michael.—Salvation by works, or salvation by faith.

THE ministry of Boos, conducted on the principles that have been exhibited in the preceding chapter, was successful in " turning many from darkness to light." He has recorded several interesting cases, of which the following may serve as examples.

A man named Michael had enjoyed for a long time a high reputation for piety, but suffered great anguish from the dread of the judgment of God. He had recourse to every possible means for quieting his conscience. He had made many pilgrimages, and more than thirty general confessions. Every year he gave to the poor two barrels of cyder, two measures of corn, and half a pig. He paid for preaching sermons, and adopted and educated destitute illegitimate children. All this was done for the purpose of obtaining forgiveness from God, and peace of mind. But Michael was much tried in his circumstances. His swine died or were stolen, and his crops were mildewed ;

so that he had nothing left for himself and his adopted children, or for the poor. Michael knew not what to think. "How is this?" he exclaimed ; "I give God the tithe of all he gives me, in alms to the poor; and yet he now takes all from me !" Sorely perplexed, he went to his minister, and stated the case. "It seems to me," he said, "as if either God has taken no pleasure in my good works, or that my works are not good. It is just as if I were Cain, with whose sacrifice God was not pleased.

Boos. How so?

Michael. Why, I have been so unfortunate. What I should otherwise have given to the poor, has been stolen, or destroyed by the rot and mildew, so that I have nothing either for others, or for myself.

Boos could hardly forbear smiling, but Michael's sorrowful looks moved his pity, and he replied : "Michael, the good works you did were, no doubt, in themselves good and praiseworthy ; but if you did them in order to merit a righteousness available before God, or to get to heaven, so that you expected to be justified and saved for your good works, and not purely of God's grace, through faith in Christ, it is no wonder that your good works have been stolen, or consumed by rot and mildew."

At these words Michael looked perplexed, and said, "Then are we not to merit heaven by our good works?"

Boos. No ; these great blessings, the pardon

of sin, grace, and eternal life, we obtain by faith in Jesus Christ, purely and solely of grace. Christ has merited these things for us by his obedience unto the death of the cross. He who believes this by the Holy Spirit, obtains and enjoys them. He who does not believe, obtains them not, even though, like yourself, he may give bacon, cyder, and corn, annually to the poor. Only think, Michael, how can any one purchase such great things, as the forgiveness of sins, heaven, and eternal life, with a pig, a barrel of cyder, and half a bushel of corn? In that case, only people of property could get to heaven, and poor creatures, who are not worth a farthing, must remain outside.

Michael. But are good works of no use?

Boos. They are of some use; if done in faith, *and with the grace of God*, they prepare us * (as in the case of the centurion Cornelius) for obtaining forgiveness and justification, and the true knowledge of Christ. For this favour is granted us freely from grace alone, through faith in Christ, and in order that all the glory may redound to God and Christ, and not to us. For if Abraham, or if Michael, were justified by works, they, and not God, would have the glory. (Romans iv. 2.)

Michael was still more astonished at this; he understood not what was said. These sayings were to him full of mystery, indeed suspicious.

* There is some obscurity in this statement of Boos. Good works, acceptable to God, are properly the fruits of faith in the Lord Jesus Christ.

Boos then took out a New Testament, and said : "You believe that this is God's word, and therefore the truth?"

Michael. Yes ; I do believe so.

Boos. Now see and hear whether Christ and his apostles have not said so. Boos then read to him John iii. 16; vi. 40; Rom. iii. 20, 30 ; Gal. ii. 16 ; Titus iii. 5. But all these passages did not calm his agitation. At last Boos came to the passage in Rom. v. 18 : "Therefore as by the offence of one, judgment came upon all men to condemnation ; even so by the righteousness of one, the free gift came upon all men unto justification of life." This at once opened Michael's eyes. "Then," said he, "do we inherit the righteousness which will avail us before God, as we inherit sin and unrighteousness from Adam?"

Boos. Yes, Michael, even so.

Michael. Now I understand it.

Boos. Do you now believe that it is so?

Michael. Yes ; I do believe.

Boos. Are you glad that you must not, and dare not seek to purchase, and to merit eternal life with a pig, a barrel of cyder, and half a bushel of corn ?

Michael. Yes, indeed ; it is a happiness that I now see this. Oh that I had come to you sooner ! Now I am relieved ; my anguish is gone ; I am happy, God be praised !

Boos. But Michael, you must not imagine that I reject good works, because I ascribe salvation to faith. My exhortation to you is, Be as diligent in good works as you have ever been.

Henceforward Michael was free from all slavish fears and anxieties. As he often said, he was happy and contented beyond expression. Soon after this, he applied to Boos for a copy of the New Testament, which he obtained, and read most diligently.

Another striking instance of the happy effects of Martin's labours, was that of Magdalene. She was a widow, who abounded in what were esteemed good works; she presented altar-clothes and other vestments to the church, but yet was one of those " who are all their lifetime subject to bondage through fear of death." "What will become of me when I die ? " was her frequent exclamation. Her confessions and prayers afforded her no relief. When she came to confess, she wept bitterly, and could only say, "I am undone !"

At last her anger rose against Boos, and she complained of him to another aged confessor that he rejected all church offerings and good works, because he often addressed her as a self-righteous person, who was always trying to make herself righteous. But on hearing a sermon from Boos, (on September 8, 1810,) she received new impressions of Divine truth ; she felt as if the discourse had been addressed exclusively to herself. "He means me !" she secretly thought, and held her head down with shame and confusion. When the sermon was

ended, she came to the confessional, and opened
her heart to Boos, shedding a flood of tears
He administered to her the consolations of the
gospel. "Only believe that Jesus died for thee,
and has made satisfaction for thy sins. Open
thy mouth and heart to receive forgiveness as
a Divine gift." From that time she found joy
and peace in believing. She bought fourteen
copies of the New Testament, and distributed
them among her relations. After having endured persecution, and faithfully confessed Him
in whom she believed, she peacefully resigned
her soul into his hands in 1816. The atmo-
sphere of heaven (says Gossner) was felt by all
who surrounded her dying bed.

A countrywoman had often come to the
minister's door, with the intention of opening
her heart to him; but her fears were too strong,
and sent her back again. At last, one day she
took courage, went to him and thanked him,
weeping, for all his sermons. Boos, who had
inferred from her behaviour at the confessional
that her conscience was in a very disturbed
state, said to her, "Though you like to hear
my sermons, and have just thanked me for
them, I fear you do not thoroughly believe
what I preach."

Countrywoman. "Oh yes; I believe all you
preach."

Boos. "I doubt it. Your agitation and the
anxiety you feel on account of your sins, con-
vince me that much unbelief still adheres to

you, and that you do not yet fully believe that God will pardon you for Christ's sake, and fill your heart with his Holy Spirit."

Weeping bitterly, the woman replied, "Alas! I am very far from being what I ought to be. I am too great a sinner for God to forgive me everything."

Boos. I am a greater sinner than you, but it has been possible for God to pardon me, and the woman who washed Christ's feet with her tears, and the Samaritan at Jacob's well, and Peter, and Paul, and the thief on the cross. It is therefore possible for him to pardon you. Think, now; you are displeasing God at this very moment by your unbelief; you are sinning before me, your minister.

She wept still more, and could not speak for weeping. She could not say again that she was too great a sinner, and that it was not possible for God to forgive her. Boos now proved to her, from many passages of Scripture, that God pardons the greatest sinners who believe in Jesus Christ; that righteousness is obtained, not by works, but by faith; that in this respect, there is no difference between a poor countrywoman, a clergyman, and a malefactor. "Therefore," said Boos, "be persuaded to receive this great gift...I tell you that God, your heavenly Father, has so loved you, that he has given you what is of more value than heaven and earth, even his only begotten Son, in all his righteousness and holiness. He will forgive you all your sins instantly, and you have nothing more to do than with open hands and heart to receive the great gift. Do you believe this?"

The tears streaming down her face, she answered with a loud voice, "I can do no otherwise; I must believe."

"Blessed art thou!" said Boos, "go in peace, thy sins are forgiven thee."

Countrywoman. "I cannot go yet; I feel as if I were in heaven. If you will allow me, I will stay a little longer. I never felt as I do now in all my life."

Accordingly, she stayed till evening, and then went away filled with that "peace of God which passeth all understanding."

Three days after she came again in great distress, and exclaimed, "I have lost my peace; I am undone; I shall scarcely be saved."

Boos. "And why so?"

Countrywoman. "Because I keep a public-house, and my husband is a drunkard, and I have a large family. I am overwhelmed with temptations, perplexities, and business; it will not do for me."

Boos smiled and said, "Now I am certain that your faith is genuine,* since in the space of only three days it has been so violently tried. Be of good cheer; let not your courage sink. If persons in all conditions of life could not believe in Christ and be saved, Jesus would never have

---

* This requires some qualification; because it is not the mere trial of faith, but the endurance of trial, that proves it to be genuine.

commanded his apostles to preach the gospel
to every creature. Had it been otherwise, he
must have said, Preach the gospel to every
creature, excepting brewers and publicans, and
women who have drunken husbands, large
families, and many customers, for they cannot
believe ;—they have no time to be saved. But
Jesus has not spoken thus ! Therefore cheer
up ; be firm, and say, ' Get thee behind me,
Satan !' "

Countrywoman. " Then I must try once
more, but I really thought it impossible for
me to be saved."

She then left Boos, with her mind once more
set at rest. Yet she often expressed a wish to
leave her family and business, and live in re-
tirement. " Not yet," said her judicious and
faithful pastor ; " remain where you are. The
apostles and first Christians retained their faith,
and love, and inward peace in the midst of
the world, and they were human beings like
you and me." This answer satisfied her, and
she pursued her calling with confidence and
joy. And she was blessed in so doing ; for
her daughters and sisters, and some of her
neighbours, were brought by her instrument-
ality to believe the gospel. And she that
watered others was watered also herself.
(Prov. xi. 25.) Her husband died in 1814.
She had then an opportunity of quitting the
business, and living retired. But she said to
herself, " I have lived here happily for five
years ; my children are still young ; I will

educate them in a Christian manner, and God
will be my husband, and their father."

Boos used every evening to assemble his
household together, and to read to them concerning faith, the new "life with Christ in
God," and the free and powerful operation of
faith working by love, when it is once en-
kindled in the heart from above, and animated
by the Spirit of the Father and the Son. The
epistles of Paul were read; and it was remarked
that if only Paul was satisfied, James would
certainly be so too.*

Boos would say to them, "God does not
first look at the sacrifice of Abel. If Cain had
been good, his offering would have been good
and acceptable to God. Let thy evil heart first
be made good by Christ, and then good works
will proceed from thy renewed nature. Ye
must be born again, and be made new men.
Then will you bring forth many fruits of faith,
love, and righteousness."

Thus Boos spoke in his own house, and in
every house which he had occasion to enter.
The people were melted into tears. They
perceived that Christ is all in all, and that
man is nothing. He then kneeled down with
them in the dust before the pierced feet of the
crucified Saviour; and gave up himself and all
those contrite and awakened souls into the
arms of the Redeemer. Then were they full

---

* Meaning apparently that whoever obeyed Paul's injunctions
to holiness, would certainly fulfil those of James.

of joy and gratitude. Thus was Boos constantly leading them away from himself, and directing them to Christ:

"Oh, those were days never to be forgotten!" says Gossner, speaking of this period. "The grace of God was manifested to all who listened to the testimony of Christ, and received it. They obtained the assurance of the forgiveness of their sins, and their adoption into the family of God; for they received the peace of God. Temptations and trials of their faith were not wanting; hence many became weak and wavering; but they were re-animated and encouraged by those who were stronger.

CHAPTER X.

Another storm—Interview with Counsellor Bertgen.

ANOTHER storm was now rising against Boos. Some of the inhabitants of Gallneukirch could not quietly listen to a preacher who was always telling them that they did not possess saving faith, and that unless they were born again, they could not see the kingdom of God. Accordingly, they lodged a complaint against Boos with the bishop and the consistory.

The bishop wrote to him with his own hand, urging him to modify his preaching ; and the Government ordered a member of the consistory, counsellor Bertgen, to obtain some information respecting Boos, as a preliminary step to a further investigation. Bertgen was vicar of Lintz, and Boos had been his chaplain for some years. The following is an account of the conversation that took place between them on January 28, 1811.

Bertgen. "Well, what have you been doing ?"

Boos. "I know of nothing."

Bertgen. "And *I* know of nothing ; but

there are very serious complaints brought against you to the consistory."

Boos. "What are they?"

Bertgen. "It is a serious matter, I assure you."

Boos. "What is it, then?—for I really know of no offence or complaints."

Bertgen. "Have you not clandestinely introduced prohibited books into the country?"

Boos. "I know of nothing of the kind."

Bertgen. "What! will you deny it? Look here. I have before me one intitled, '*The Hidden Life with Christ in God.*' A very unfit publication for common people. For, in the first place, it is unintelligible, unless the Holy Ghost explain it to them. Secondly, it does away with all diligence and effort. Thirdly, it only makes enthusiasts, fanatics, pietists."

Boos. "In the first place, I did not introduce the book clandestinely, but the Bavarian carrier brought two hundred copies openly through the city gates. They were weighed at the custom-house, and submitted to the censorship; and as there was no prohibition, I received them without hesitation. I have before distributed this little work in Wallneukirch and Peuerbach, when I was your curate. As to the book itself, the author is a good Catholic; the contents are Catholic; and any one who has tasted and experienced something of the influence of the Holy Spirit, and of the inward life with Christ in God, can understand it; however mystical and unintelligible it may be to the merely natural man. I have circulated this book for many years ; and many thousand persons have read it with delight and profit ; and it is continually inquired for. Why is it now, for the first time, complained of ?"

Bertgen. "People do not understand it. I scarcely understand it myself."

Boos. "Among all classes there are spiritually-minded persons, like old Simeon and Anna, in whose hearts the Holy Spirit dwells, and they often see what the learned and wise fail to discern. Simeon in a poor infant saw the Messiah ; and so did Anna, with all the pious simple-hearted people in Jerusalem, who 'waited for the consolation of Israel.' So it was with the wise men from the east. The scribes and high priest, Herod and his people, educated and intelligent though they might be, saw nothing in Jesus after he had been three-and-thirty years among them, and had made the blind to see, the deaf to hear, and the lame to walk, and had raised the dead. ' The natural man,' says St. Paul, 'receiveth not the things of the Spirit of God, for they are foolishness unto him. But he that is spiritual judgeth all things, yet he himself is judged of no man.' (1 Cor. ii. 14, 15.)"

Bertgen became more calm and thoughtful ; but yet advised Boos not to circulate the book any more; for the vicar-general had told him that it was prohibited at Rome.

Boos. "That may be. As to circulating it, I can give that up."

Bertgen. "Why do you always preach so much about a living faith?"

Boos. "Because we have a superabundance of a dead, unloving, inoperative faith, while in all quarters there is a deficiency of living faith. Moreover, a living faith leads me and my parishioners to the forgiveness of sins, peace of conscience, the Holy Spirit, and grateful love; it leads to all good works, and finally to eternal life. Faith is the first article in the catechism: the first command; and without faith it is impossible to please God, to live holily, and to die happily. Faith, in short, saves us; why, then, should I not speak of faith?"

Bertgen. "But why do you *always* speak of it?"

Boos. "My sermons will furnish sufficient evidence that I do not speak of faith *exclusively*. But I confess that I *often* preach about it, and for the following reasons:

"(1.) A countryman in my parish hung himself simply from unbelief and despair.

"(2.) I meet with an amazing number of anxious and desponding people at the confessional.

"(3.) Living faith is far from being possessed by every one. It is not so general in the universal church as people imagine; for the faith of the head and the lips is not true faith.

"(4.) I cannot impart peace and comfort to distressed and anxious sinners with anything

but the living faith that God for Christ's sake
is ready to forgive their sins, on their repenting
and believing. This I know from my own
experience and that of others.

" (5.) Inward Christianity must precede that
which is outward, as good fruit proceeds
from a good tree; and inward Christianity
consists in faith, hope, and love. For both our
Lord Jesus Christ and the apostle Paul affirm
that what does not proceed from faith and love
is worth nothing. Outward Christianity must
proceed from the inward, as well as our good
works and virtues; and where it is not so,
there is no living faith."

Bertgen. "Do not always say, ' *living faith.*'
People will be led to think they must believe
with the body; that they must use their physical and corporeal powers for the purpose."

Boos. " *With the body!* By no means. The
phrase only serves to distinguish it from a
mere faith of the lips, and the letter without
love, and the works of love. ' With the heart
man believeth unto righteousness.' "

Bertgen. "But why did you say in your
sermons that those who had living faith among
your parishioners, might be easily contained
in the sacristy ? "

Boos. "I said that in the excitement of my
feelings, when I divided my parishioners into
four classes ; namely—

" (1.) Those who were devoted to pleasure
and were unconcerned.

" (2.) The self-righteous.

" (3.) The alarmed and troubled.

" (4.) Those who have a living, devout, restful, joyous, saving faith. And to this latter class 'many are called, but few chosen;' and if brought to the test and numbered, I said they would scarcely fill the sacristy; but whether that be so or not, God alone knows."

Bertgen. "Did not this offend the people greatly?"

Boos. "Not so much as you seem to suppose. Most of them love me, and I converse with them, all the year round, in a free, unconstrained manner, like a father with his children, as I used to do when I was your curate. And besides, if what a preacher says be true and evident, why should he care whether it pleases the people? 'Woe to him of whom all men speak well.' Christ also says, 'Narrow is the way that leadeth unto life, and few there be that find it.'—'Many are called, but few chosen.' If he was so plain spoken as to call his hearers whited sepulchres, hypocrites, vipers, (Matt. xxiii.) may not a preacher venture to say that there are few who live according to Christ's mind and doctrine? Lastly, our sacristy is not so small; for it can hold above a hundred persons."

Bertgen (after a pause). "And what has your curate Rehberger been doing? for he is accused as well as yourself."

Boos. "He does as I do; he assists me in preaching faith, hope, and love. The people and I are perfectly satisfied with him; he is laborious, unblameable, and zealous."

Shortly afterwards Rehberger entered the room. Bertgen looked very grave and said, in rather an excited tone, "This is indeed a very serious business! Grievous complaints are made against you both to the consistory, and I am commissioned to examine you. You must bring me all your books and sermons, and give an exact account of your mode of teaching."

Boos. "We are ready to undergo the strictest examination, and are thankful to God and the consistory for having sent you, our best friend, to be our examiner. We are glad to be called to confess our faith before our superiors. We will faithfully and with pleasure lay before you all our discourses; for we are not ashamed of the gospel: and we will give you the best answers and explanations in our power."

Bertgen was now calmer in his manner, yet not quite so cordial as before; but rather reserved and captious. From that time he began to prepare himself for conducting the examination, and read, as he afterward told Boos, several books on the subject of justification. While reading these authors his mind became so enlightened that for three nights he could not sleep for joy.

On returning home and reflecting on what had passed at this interview, Boos engaged in earnest prayer, especially on Bertgen's behalf, (not from any fear of the consequences to himself, but from the spirit of Christian benevolence,) that his mind might be enlightened, and delivered from all prejudices against the truth. The sequel will show that his prayers were not in vain.

On February 7, 1811, Bertgen came again to Gallneukirch. His first words to Boos were, "I could not sleep the whole of last night; I have been reading the Council of Trent on Justification; I never, in my whole life, felt so much pleasure on coming to Gallneukirch as I do to-day." "So much the better," said Boos; "the inquiry will be more in our favour." "Do not talk about the inquiry," said the commissioner, "I am come merely for a friendly conversation, that I may be able to stop the mouths of the censorious, and prevent them from annoying you."

After listening to the explanations of Boos, Bertgen desired the two curates to withdraw, and then sitting down with Boos, asked him to state his views of the doctrine of justification. "I understand it," Boos replied, "in the same way that the Council of Trent explains and understands it:" and he quoted several passages from chapters 7 and 8.

Bertgen then asked what disposition he thought was required on the part of man for this justification. Boos replied, (referring again to the Council of Trent,) "the disposition manifested by Cornelius, (Acts x.) by Peter in the ship, by the penitent woman at the feet of Jesus, by the thief on the cross. Men must be poor in spirit, must acknowledge, feel, repent of, and confess their sinfulness; must forsake their sins; and believe that God for Christ's sake will not impute our sins to us, but forgive us, and impute to us the righteousness of God and Christ which Adam had lost for himself and us, freely and of grace for the merits of Christ."

Bertgen. "And is this the doctrine you preach?"

Boos. "Yes; my sermons, which I submit to your inspection, will prove it."

Bertgen sprang from his seat, and lifting his hands, said, with strong emotion, "What fools! to call this heresy—the most consolatory doctrine in all theology! They ought rather to be thankful that you preach it so decidedly."

Boos. "Persons who understand us, do thank us most cordially. But it is not so with all; and, like the Ephesians in the market-place, they cry out, 'Diana! Diana!' without knowing what and wherefore. But we must have patience with them 'till the day dawn, and the day-star arise in their hearts.'"

Bertgen then took up a manuscript of Boos containing the fifteen propositions which his adversaries regarded as heretical. He listened patiently to every explanation, and at the close, said to Boos, "Make yourself easy; I will defend your '*living faith*' against your enemies, in the consistory. I perceive that the truth of the case is totally different from what they and the consistory supposed it to be."

This interview lasted from eight o'clock to twelve. At four o'clock Bertgen set off for Lintz, taking with him the sermons and other papers which had been put into his hands. He sent Boos word back by the coachman that " he might sleep in peace."

CHAPTER XI.

Boos defends his cause—Appears before the vicar-general.

At the first sitting of the consistory after the conversation with Boos narrated in the fore-going chapter, Bertgen gave a report of all that had passed on that occasion, and pleaded in behalf of Boos with so much address, that all further proceedings seemed to be quashed. But the complainants were not to be thus silenced. They reproached Bertgen with hav-ing misunderstood or misrepresented Boos's sentiments, and accused him of partiality, and even of heresy. Nor did they stop here ; they harassed the consistory with their accusations, and represented Boos as a dangerous man, who must be got rid of at any cost. In conse-quence, he was cited to appear before the vicar-general, Ferdinand Mayr, on the 12th March, 1811. The following account is given by himself in a letter to one of his friends:—

"I wrote, not long ago, to inform you, that owing to the exertions of Bertgen, everything had been comfortably settled; but it was only a truce. On the 3rd of this month (March) I received from the vicar-general a letter in the following terms:—

"'Reverend Sir,—I hear that several of your parishioners have been perplexed by the doctrine you have taught at Gallneukirch, and have consulted other pastors on various points which were not clear to them. As the matter is one of extreme importance, I wish to have a conversation with you upon it, at the earliest opportunity you may have of coming to Lintz. If you can fix a day on which you could conveniently come, I should prefer it. Meanwhile, I request that you would either not touch on the points of doctrine which have excited doubts in your public discourses, or refer to them with the utmost delicacy and prudence.

"'I am, etc.'

"In consequence of this communication, I appointed yesterday, the 12th of March, for the conference. I sent the letter on the 5th to Bertgen, and asked his opinion whether I should venture to present myself before this new inquisition. His answer was as follows :—

"'Keep yourself at ease, and take care of your health. You must not give up preaching, though I need not say it must be with proper caution. As for the rest, comply with the contents of the letter. I shall be glad to see you, and speak with you beforehand.'

"When I saw Bertgen yesterday, at seven in the morning, he said, What do you think is the reason why you are again cited to appear?

I replied that I did not know. ' Why,' said he, 'Brunner, formerly minister at Pöstlingberg, has sent your friendly letter, with your propositions (which you wrote the day before I came to Gallneukirch) to the vicar-general, with a number of charges, so that the vicar and the whole chapter are again alarmed.'

" After some further conversation we went to the court. The vicar would not undertake the examination alone, but brought as his coadjutor, the aged canon Reiccessi, an Italian. They began with reading the letter which I addressed to the vicar-general on March 4th. Various expressions were objected to ; for instance, that I doubted whether all men possessed living faith in Christ and his gospel. No one (they maintained) was deficient in faith, but only in works. The term '*living*' applied to faith, was strongly reprobated; they proposed to substitute '*working by love.*' This point I can concede to them. Then three hours were spent in examining the propositions which were to be tried by the standard of the decrees of the Council of Trent ; but we could not agree as to the result. I quoted Scripture on my side, and they on theirs ; but which party had the victory was undecided. At last we rose, and I began with tears to confess my faith in Jesus Christ, and entreated them not to disturb the belief of one who must soon die, nor my dying parishioners : for we all rendered only an imperfect obedience, and therefore came to our death-beds as sinners, and needed

Christ, not as a mere supplement to make up the defects of our doings, but required him wholly, with all his merits ; and that with any other faith than this, I could not venture to prepare myself and my parishioners for a happy death. This, and much more, I said with many tears. Then one took me by the right hand, and the other by the left, and tried to comfort me, by saying, that I might use this faith for myself, and my dying parishioners, for our mutual comfort, but that for the healthy, and such as were likely to live, if this faith were publicly preached it would create a disturbance. It would become me, therefore, to take suitable opportunities for presenting the subject to the people more simply, and in a less offensive manner. They said that the esteem they had felt for me before this investigation, so far from being lessened, had rather increased, but I ought to be on my guard against mysticism, lest I should fall into fanaticism, etc.

" But to sum up the whole, it was evident that they knew neither the Father, nor the Son, nor us, nor the faith in which, through grace, we stand. St. Paul, for instance, they thought, speaks in his Epistle to the Romans, merely of the ceremonial law, and not concerning the whole Mosaic law, divine and moral. The veil is still upon their hearts. They consider Sailer as the greatest enthusiast and fanatic in all Germany ; this they told me three times to my face. You may imagine how I was pained to hear it. I told you long ago, that we had been greatly mistaken about these men. Christ is too great a gift for them; their heart is too narrow.

"After this grievous conflict at Augsburg, I went to dine with Bertgen, who comforted me as a father would his child. In answer to his inquiries, I gave him the details of all that had occurred. He said, ' To-morrow I will attack them, and call them to account for not having believed me, and for giving ear, instead, to such knaves as Brunner and Parzer, who merely sought to promote their own base ends, by bringing charges against me and you.'

"What has transpired in the consistory to-day I know not. . . . . According to my opponents, no man knows anything of peace and joy in the Holy Ghost, and he who professes that he knows any such thing is a fanatic, or an enthusiast . . . . The whole country, they say, needs renovation; the Catholic religion is on the eve of extinction, and Lutheranism is gaining the ascendency; and how lamentable will that be ! Bertgen is aware of all this, and will do his utmost to defend us; but he stands alone. The whole country is disturbed as in 1797. In my parish, where they are most quiet, a thousand persons are ready to go to Lintz, and defend us against our accusers; for they all see that Brunner is only actuated by the mean motive of wishing to get possession of my parish."

CHAPTER XII.

Professor Sailer.

ONE powerful voice, however, was raised in behalf of Boos; that of his ancient instructor and friend, professor Sailer, a distinguished preacher and writer, who was deservedly held in high esteem, both by Protestants and Catholics. This excellent prelate had heard with great satisfaction of the zeal and piety of Boos, and of the generous manner in which Bertgen had undertaken to plead his cause. His sentiments are fully expressed in the following letter to Bertgen, dated May 11, 1811 :—

"I can be silent no longer. The manliness, prudence, and love for apostolic Christianity which you have displayed in defending our friend Boos, when so violently assailed on matters relating to his faith and conscience, have so filled me with delight and with esteem and affection for you, that I cannot be sufficiently thankful to God, and must pour forth the feelings of my heart to you.

"There is one holy catholic faith, but this catholic faith may be either—1, mechanically and outwardly learned ; or, 2, scholastically apprehended ; or, 3, spiritually received.

"Boos is a spiritual catholic Christian. What to the mechanical Christian is the mere letter, and to the scholastic Christian nothing but notions, is to him spirit and life. His disposition is spiritually catholic; for he receives and judges of all the doctrines of the Catholic church from a spiritual point of view, in their relation to the inner life—their influence on the heart—their devotional tendency. Whatever has no beneficial effect on the inner man, is nothing to him. For this reason, the scholastic Christians charge him with heresy; and the mechanical Christians are afraid of him. To the latter, his expressions are offensive; and it must be admitted that many of them are not perfectly correct in mere formal strictness, but, tried by the standard of the Spirit, they are so."

After quoting several passages from the Council of Trent, Sailer goes on to say, "When Boos speaks of good works, after justification, a distinction must be noted. 1. If these good works are considered as proceeding from the man himself, and altogether his own, they are certainly tainted with selfishness, and therefore have no intrinsic worth in God's sight. 2. But if these good works are considered as performed by the Spirit of Christ, in and through the man, they are certainly wrought in God, are precious in his sight, and have a Divine value; but this value comes from the Spirit of Christ, which rules and reigns in the will that is animated by Christ; these good works are good from the applied merits of Christ.

"But the most pious person is still a man, and does not always allow the good Spirit to possess and govern him. Often selfishness or an evil spirit actuates him. Hence it is desirable that the just, or justified person, should not rely on his good works, for he would rely on something which has no stability ; but let him found his confidence on God, on Christ, on the Spirit of Christ ; and this edifice will stand firm. This is also the doctrine of the fathers. ' The just shall live by faith.'

"Therefore, if Boos is brought before an ecclesiastical court, every thing depends on what kind of Christians his judges are. 1. If they are *mechanical*, they will condemn Boos as an *enthusiast*. 2. If they are *scholastic*, they will 'pronounce him to be a *heretic*. But he is no heretic, since he not only adheres to the communion of the Catholic church, but embraces with his *faith* all the revelations of God, with his *hope* all the promises of God, and with his *love* all the dealings of God. Therefore his faith, hope, and love are truly Catholic.

"Boos is no enthusiast, for he does not regard the works of selfishness or of the imagination as proceeding from the Holy Spirit, but what is manifestly good, in faith and love, wrought by and through God. What the Spirit of Christ manifestly works in man according to the Scriptures, that he ascribes with humble gratitude to the Holy Spirit."

"Moreover, I would rather die than condemn a man who possesses so many distinguished

gifts of the Spirit—whom God has so wonderfully guided — who has awakened so many
thousand persons to repentance, faith, and
piety — who, by his devotion and humility
amidst persecution and suffering, has shown
himself to be a true servant of Christ—and
whose shoe-latchet the wisest and best men of
his time do not think themselves worthy to
unloose. I say, I would rather die, than condemn such a man, merely for single expressions, which manifestly are susceptible of an
orthodox meaning, and to which he is not
obstinately attached.

" I am now entering my sixtieth year, and
I should tremble to appear before God's judg-
ment-seat, if I did not, in the most emphatic
language, declare before my death that the
great cause of the pious Boos is of God! For
it consists in the following particulars :

" 1. No man is justified who is destitute of
a faith that works by love.

" 2. But faith cannot work by love, as long
as it possesses no life in itself.

" 3. Faith can only be vital, through God,
through Christ, through the Spirit of Christ.

" These three positions are—1, purely Christian ; 2, purely Catholic ; and 3, the leading
points in the cause of Boos. Everything else
is unimportant ; or, if interpreted in accordance with these positions, unobjectionable.

" Now, as the cause of Boos is a truly good
one ; as every bishop is under obligation not
to surrender the good cause of Christianity

either to the blind zeal of the mechanical Christians, or to the proud zeal of the scholastic Christians, but to preserve it unimpaired to the day of the Lord; and since God has chosen you to be the instrument of rescuing and preserving the good cause; and you alone in the whole diocese are intimately acquainted with Boos; and since you have admitted the truth into your inmost soul,—I bless you for it, and entreat you to exert all your prudence, courage, and love, that a man so actuated as Boos is by the Spirit of Christ, may be no further annoyed, either in his person or his field of labour. For if his faith in Christ be not endangered, he will be quite ready to give up expressions which are not essential to his views. In the name of every Christian, I thank you for having spoken in behalf of Boos, and for not refusing to share in the odium that lies upon him. The Lord God will reward you for it.

"MICHAEL SAILER."

Bertgen acquainted Boos with the contents of this letter, which afforded him the most lively satisfaction. Such affection for himself, and zeal for the truth, were a cordial to his spirit. The Christian needs the sympathy of his brethren. In proportion as he is disowned by the world, he claims a place in the hearts of his fellow-disciples. Boos valued the more highly the esteem of Sailer and Bertgen, because a large majority of the clergy in the diocese of Lintz looked upon him with a prejudiced eye, and many of them cherished an implacable hatred against him. In such a position, and exposed to continual attacks, he was rejoiced to meet with those who entered into his views, and did not hesitate to share the opprobrium to which his own character was subjected. He took the earliest opportunity of expressing to Sailer the satisfaction and comfort he had derived from reading his letter, in the following lines :—

" Thanks, more than I can express to you, my dear father, for your precious letter to Bertgen and myself! May the Lord reward you! It came just at the right time; for the blind zeal of the scholastics had accused me afresh to the bishop, who, about six weeks ago, became vicar-general, instead of archdeacon Mayr. The bishop would have made me undergo another inquisition; but Bertgen, fortified by your letter, opposed him heroically. The bishop, however, means to make a visitation, and, on that occasion, to hear the parties on both sides, and then either to confirm me anew, as Catholic, or reject me as uncatholic. I shall shortly request this visitation from the bishop, in conjunction with Bertgen. Unfortunately, two parties have been formed. Some say, ' Boos is a good man ;' others, ' Not so, he is a Lutheran.' It is, therefore, our earnest wish and request, that, before the visitation, you would write a letter to the bishop, of similar purport to that you wrote to Bertgen.

The bishop values, loves, and honours your person and writings extremely. One word from you, in behalf of the cause which affects my faith and conscience, would give the death-blow to all the accusations of the mechanical and scholastic Christians. If, then, it be possible, do me this act of kindness, for I am suffering much at present, both in mind and body. On the 23rd of this month, while engaged at the confessional, I broke a blood-vessel, and, up to this time, expectorate blood, and am very much reduced ; probably my end is near. On the other hand, my enemies rage and rave, and daily instigate my parishioners more and more against me and my religious views. Yesterday, the 26th of May, there was a great concourse. Bertgen and Herzog came to see me on hearing of my dangerous state. After Bertgen had performed mass, three hundred of the parishioners came, in a tumultuous manner, and demanded an audience with him. At first he was alarmed, but when he found that they only wanted him to befriend their pastor, and protect him against his opponents, and prevent his removal from them, he took courage, and assured them he would do all in his power. Then there is another party, who are loud and violent against these persons and myself, and whom nothing will satisfy but the bishop's coming to investigate the matter afresh, and finally to give his decision. My constant prayer is, ' Lord, enter not into judgment with me.' But it is the Lord's will that I, a miserable sinner, should bear his name from one tribunal to another. Gladly, like Moses, I would let another go in my stead, but there is no help for it; I must go for the fifty-sixth time. The way is toilsome; and, weakened as I am by loss of blood, I need a Simon to help me bear the cross, and a napkin to wipe away the sweat. I have copied, with tears of joy, your beautiful and excellent letter . . . . I perceive that you thoroughly understand the question relating to my faith and conscience. There is, as you say, only one holy Catholic faith; but this may be, 1, *mechanically* and *outwardly* learned; or, 2, *scholastically* apprehended; or, 3, received *spiritually*. I myself have been in all these three classes. In my childhood I was a long while in the first; in my youth, and when I first entered the clerical office, I was in the second; and, at a later period, by God's grace, after many inward and outward mortifications, I came into the third class; and from that, through being misunderstood, I am come into the fourth, that of the inquisition and exile."

. . . . . " While writing this I have been seized with a fainting fit, after an hæmorrhage. On coming to myself again, I asked my conscience whether I had reason to fear before God's tribunal, on account of my preaching faith in Christ; and the answer was, ' At God's tribunal thou wilt come off easily, on account of thy preaching Christ, but not so at a human tribunal.' (Oh, how should I rejoice to die at this very moment!)—I also asked myself whether I was not to blame for conducting myself in a strange manner in this affair. But here I could not reproach myself. ' Yet herein am I not justified.' The imprudent expressions for which men will not forgive me, God and Christ will forgive freely. I am, in all respects, a sinner; but as to my preaching faith in Christ, I am not conscious of any other sin than that of not having preached Christ more earnestly; but I believe and hope, that, through him, this and all my other sins will be forgiven, and I shall die peacefully, like a child. . . . . . . Bertgen again expressed his wish yesterday, that you would come here in the vacation. Your presence would have a decisive effect on the proceedings against me. Pray come! . . . Bertgen said, yesterday, that the whole consistory is at present a chaos and a nonentity. No one member of it loves or understands the rest. Oh that this chaos might believe in Christ, and become united to him!"

CHAPTER XIII.

Disturbances at Gallneukirch—Public dispute—Sermon of Boos.

In the face of all opposition, Boos pursued his work ; but his calmness and perseverance only increased the virulence of his enemies. The agitation on all sides became more violent, till, at last, the two parties came to an open contest, not without danger of bloodshed. Some of the ringleaders were apprehended, and sentenced to a week's imprisonment.

Among the persons who took a prominent part in these proceedings was Saul Höllinger, one of the magistrates, who went to such a length as to declaim vehemently against Boos in the market-place. Yet he was a person who, in general estimation, passed for a very religious man. For half a year he had been vilifying Boos, and charging him with repudiating good works, though he only taught that sinners could not be justified by them, but freely by grace, for Christ's sake, and that good works must follow from faith and grateful love in childlike humility. But Höllinger could not comprehend this. One of his charges against Boos was, that the lamp, which used to be kept constantly burning in the church, had been suffered to go out, and was not relighted. " Is not that a sign," said Höllinger, " that the light of the true faith has been extinguished ?"

" Do not talk so absurdly," replied a country justice ; " what do I care about the light in the lamp, whether it burn or not ? Our minister has kindled the light of living faith in our hearts ; and that is more delightful to me than the oil light in the church lamp. Of what use is the light in the lamp, if the light of faith and love do not burn in the heart ?"

Höllinger. Why, he says himself that faith has become extinct among us ! Have you never heard of his saying that the sacristy would hold all his parishioners who possessed true faith ?

The Justice. Yes, and with truth. Perhaps neither I nor you would have a right to enter the sacristy : for, oh, my brother, it is no little thing to say that we have living faith in Christ. It is not a thing to be picked up by chance in the market-place. For my part, I do not think the worse of him for speaking in that manner.

" Nor I ! nor I !" was uttered by many voices from a crowd of between two and three hundred bystanders.

" And when you once understand him aright," continued the justice, " like myself and a hundred others, you too will not think the worse of him."

Höllinger. But does he not call our good works " dung and dross ? "

The Justice. And rightly ; but he only means works of selfishness and self-righteousness, of which, like the Pharisees, we vaunt and boast ; and these Paul also " counted as dung" as soon as he was enlightened. (Phil. iii. 8.) My brother ! you are still destitute of the true light, and of a perfect understanding. You do not understand the minister, or you would not talk so.

Höllinger. Well ! do you keep to your faith, and I will keep to mine.

The Justice. Yes ! so I mean to do.

And thus the dispute ended; but the people thought that the justice had the best of it.

A few days after, Boos preached a sermon which, under God's blessing, was the means of converting some of his bitterest enemies, and among others, this Saul Höllinger. His text was Matt. xxviii. 18—20, "And Jesus came and spake unto them, saying, All power is given unto me in heaven and in earth. Go ye therefore, and teach all nations, baptizing them in the name of the Father, and of the Son, and of the Holy Ghost," etc. The following is a tolerably correct outline of it :—

"Jesus of Nazareth, whom the world crucified, is the Lord of heaven and earth. 1. He says himself, ' All power is given unto me in heaven and earth.' 2. He sends his messengers, his apostles, with his commands, not merely to one village, town, country, or people, but to all

villages, towns, lands, and people throughout
the world.

" He is, therefore, manifestly the Lord and
King of heaven and earth. 1, Because he
sends his messengers and commands into all
the world. 2. Because through them he has
commanded the whole world, all kings and
princes—all citizens and peasants, to believe on
him—to be baptized in his name, and to observe all the things he has commanded them.
3. Because he threatens the whole world, that
if they do not believe in him they shall be
condemned.

" The whole world is, in God's sight, one
enormous sinner ; and if she does not believe in
him, does not repent, is not baptized, and ob-
serves not the things he has commanded, this
enormous sinner is, and will be, condemned.

" To believe in Jesus Christ, therefore, is not
an affair which may be left undone, as, for
instance, a pilgrimage ; no, it is a command, it
must be done. If thou wilt be saved, if thou
wilt not be condemned, thou must believe that
Jesus died for thee—that he, by his death on
the cross, has gained for thee the forgiveness
of sins and everlasting life ; and that he will
grant thee his righteousness, dwell in thee by
his Holy Spirit, and enable thee to fulfil all
God's commandments.

" ' He who believeth not on the Son, shall
not see life, but the wrath of God abideth on
him.' Consequently, we preachers are not at
liberty to preach what we please. No ; we

are servants, and, as such, must preach and teach what the Lord has commanded us. Woe to us if we know his command, and yet do not preach the gospel. For a servant who knows his Lord's will, and does it not, shall be beaten with many stripes. 'Woe is me,' says St. Paul, 'if I preach not the gospel.' I must. Woe also to us preachers if we do not preach the gospel to the world; though the world gives us no thanks, and rewards us only with its unbelief. In all ages the world can endure any thing rather than the gospel. John preached it, and the world beheaded him. Jesus preached it, and the world crucified him. The apostles preached it, and the world put them to death. It is, therefore, a hard lot to be an evangelist, a preacher of the gospel. If a man preach not the gospel to the world, he is condemned by God and Christ. If he does preach it, he is condemned by the world."

(Here a great part of the congregation wept aloud, for it was generally known that their minister was on the point of being condemned; and some said that he would be burnt.)

"But what is the gospel which Christ has commanded us to preach? And why does the world not receive the gospel?

"The gospel is the most joyful and consolatory news to the world; for it announces to a sinful world the glad tidings that 'God has so loved the world, that he has given'—not gold and silver, not a kingdom, but something much greater—'his only begotten Son,' with all his wisdom, righteousness, holiness, and merits, (1 Cor. i. 30.) And the world which, without him, is nothing, and can do nothing, has at first nothing to do but to receive the great gift by faith. It is not I, but Christ who says this. John iii. 16. . . . .

"There is a great difference between the law and the gospel. . . . The law says, Thou must do this, or thou art cursed and condemned. It threatens, drives, and terrifies, but gives us no strength, no love, no pleasure, no life for performing. It points out the way, but does not enable to walk in it. It settles no reckoning, pays no debt. And since even the most pious man does not fulfil every requirement of the law, through innate depravity and weakness, such a one on his death-bed has often the greatest anxiety and fear.

"But here comes the gospel with consolation, and says to the despairing sinner, Despair not, but look, like the dying thief, to the crucified One—or, like the penitent woman, throw thyself at his feet—believe and trust in him, then thou shalt be admitted into Paradise, like the former ; and be told, like the latter, that 'thy sins are forgiven thee.' 'He is the Lamb of God, which taketh away the sin of the world;' and since thou art a part, though a small part, of the world, he will take away thy sins, and at once justify and save thee. . .

"But why will not the world receive the gospel ?

"1. Because it knows neither the Father

nor the Son ; as Christ says, (John xvi. 3.)
The apostles preached the gospel to the world,
and they thrust them out of the synagogues,
slew them, and believed that in doing so they
did God service. · The god of this world
blinded their eyes, that they saw not the clear
light of the gospel. ' The ox knoweth his
owner, and the ass his master's crib, but Israel
doth not know me.' 2. Because it knows not
itself. The world knows not that out of Christ
it is nothing but sin, condemned and lost—
knows not, therefore, that it is redeemed by
Christ. 3. Because it knows not the Scriptures. It allows itself no time to read them.
The farmer goes to his field—the citizen to his
business—no one reads the Scriptures, and
before the eyes of almost all there is a veil,
so that, though they have eyes, they see not.
4. The world will not allow itself to be a sinner
and worth nothing. But this is what the gospel
pronounces it to be. 5. The gospel puts down
all self-righteousness. But the world is righteous in its own esteem. 6. The gospel rejects
all pride and haughtiness, and says, ' Unless ye
become as little children, ye cannot enter the
kingdom of heaven.'· But to become thus little
does not suit the world. 7. The gospel
abjures all sinful pleasures. But all these the
world loves. Hence arises its enmity against
the gospel. But I pray you, in Christ's stead,
reject not the gospel, this message of consolation, for what else can give you peace and joy
either in life or in death ?"

"Our Father, who art in heaven! thou know-est what passes on earth, and in my parish of Gallneukirch. Open the eyes of my beloved parishioners, that thy name and thy Son's name may be known and sanctified, that thy kingdom may come to us, and thy will be done, as in heaven, so on earth."

The effects of this discourse were very extra-ordinary. The pious part of the congregation were delighted, and many said they would not have missed hearing it for a thousand florins. Others, who till then had been insensible to the claims of religion, or had satisfied themselves with a dull routine of outward observances, were roused by it from their spiritual lethargy. Very many who had previously been opposed to the preacher and his doctrine, were dis-armed of their prejudices. One of the most respectable parishioners, who had often lodged complaints against Boos with the bishop, came immediately after the sermon, confessed his sins, and with tears intreated forgiveness. This was no other than Saul Höllinger, of whom mention has been made above. He was not present at the morning sermon, of which we have given an abstract, but his wife and son were there. On coming home they exclaimed in the fulness of their hearts, "O my husband! O my father! how we wish you had heard the sermon this morning." "Why so?" "We tell you," they replied, "you are, and will be, con-demned, unless you believe the minister and his words, and give up your opposition." He replied rather warmly, "Go away! the minister cannot condemn me, nor can you." "Oh," said his wife again, " that you had heard him to-day! Does not the minister, does not the gospel itself say, ' He that believeth not is condemned ?'"

As his wife and son importuned him thus with tears, he became thoughtful, restless, and perplexed. To obtain satisfaction, he sat down with his New Testament and lighted on the passage in Rom. ix. 30—33, " What shall we say then ? That the gentiles, which followed not after righteousness, have attained to righteousness, even the righteousness which is of faith. But Israel, which followed after the law of righteousness, hath not attained to the law of righteousness. Wherefore ? Because they sought it not by faith, but as it were by the works of the law. For they stumbled at that stumblingstone. As it is written, Behold, I lay in Sion a stumblingstone and rock of offence: and whosoever believeth on him shall not be confounded."

On reading this passage he seemed as if struck by a flash of lightning; he saw himself to be one who had stumbled at that stumblingstone. He perceived that he had hitherto lived like the Jews ; that is, he had attempted to gain a righteousness that would avail before God, not by faith in Christ, but by his own works. But the hour was come. "Wife!" he all at once exclaimed, "now I have found it." "What?" said she, " What?" "Why, that the minister

was right. Neither I nor you belong to the
people in the sacristy, as he once told us it
would contain- all the people who had living
faith. We must be numbered with the self-
righteous in the nave. We have hitherto
sought to be justified by our own works, and
have not received the righteousness of God by
faith in Christ; but, like the Jews, have rejected it. Only look here, and read! Now I
understand the minister. I now see that he
was blameless, and yet I persecuted and calumniated him. God forgive me, for I knew not
what I did!"

"God be praised!" said his wife, "that you
now understand one another." "But," said he,
"I will go directly to the minister, and ask his
forgiveness." To which his wife assented, lest
he should change his mind.

Accordingly, about three o'clock in the afternoon, Höllinger came to the parsonage. The
minister was alarmed, for he was not aware
that the wolf was changed into a lamb. "Now,"
thought he, "we shall have another explosion!"
But what was his surprise when Höllinger embraced him with the utmost affection, and entreated pardon for all he had done against him.
He then acquainted Boos with the impression
made on his wife and son by the morning sermon,
and how he had been led by their conversation
to reflect on his past conduct and read the
Scriptures. Having a New Testament with
him, he turned to the passage in the Romans,
and requested Boos to explain it. He was highly

delighted to find his minister's interpretation agree with his own.

Höllinger now took every opportunity of making known the gospel. He also went to Lintz several times, and acknowledged his previous ignorance and mistaken notions to the bishop and some of the magistrates. But he was not very cordially received; several persons were ready to exclaim, "Thou art beside thyself; thou art an enthusiast."

He was afterwards one of six deputies from the parish who had an audience with the emperor at Lintz, and petitioned him to protect their minister, and prevent his removal from them.

CHAPTER XIV.

Decision of the consistory—Renewed testimony of Sailer.

ALL classes—people, priests, and bishops—were interested in the decision of Boos' case. His friends, especially Sailer and Bertgen, used their utmost endeavours to counteract the misrepresentations that were spread abroad respecting him. The former wrote to bishop Sigmund von Hohenwart (who had succeeded bishop Gall in the diocese of Lintz) to lay before him the true state of things ; and Bertgen advised Boos to take the same step, which he did with his usual candour and frankness.

The bishop cited him to appear before him. He immediately complied with the requisition, and made an avowal of his faith, and of his determination to persist in it. The prelate appeared satisfied with his replies, assembled the members of the consistory on June 5, 1811, and laid before them Sailer's letter, and that of Boos. They came, in consequence, to the following resolution :—

"The Episcopal Consistory having taken into consideration the language and proceedings of Martin Boos, which have offended some of his parishioners and occasioned the late investigation, are ready to admit, in consequence of the explanations given by the aforesaid, that he has taught no error nor dangerous doctrines, and that he has been free from bad intentions, but has been misunderstood. At the most he is to be reprehended for a too ardent zeal, and for explaining in a too exclusive manner the principles of the Catholic faith. As he has received suitable admonitions on all these points, the complainants may rest satisfied, both with respect to his discourses and the manner in which their zealous and irreproachable minister will fulfil his functions."

When this decision had been communicated to Boos, he called a meeting of the parties who had complained against him, in the hope of producing a better state of feeling towards himself. But his efforts were unsuccessful. They only said that they would consult with father Conrad and the priest Brunner, who were, in fact, the prime movers of the proceedings against him.

Bishop Sailer having received a copy of the decision of the consistory, and foreseeing that fresh troubles would arise, wrote to Bertgen as follows:—" The decision of the consistory is moderate, Christian, and just; but they must not place too much confidence in this apparent calm. It is evident that Boos has displayed extraordinary delicacy and prudence, and that his adversaries are animated by a totally different spirit. They try to find heresies and offences where none exist. Carried away by the force of prejudice, they are eager to condemn Boos, and leave nothing undone to gain their ends. Their rancour is constantly increasing, and, having failed in their first attempt, they will circulate new calumnies and neglect no means of gaining influence over the bishop. If the bishop maintains his firmness, they will endeavour to deceive and circumvent the superior authorities. I know all their artifices by my own experience, and their treatment of Boos in 1796, as well as many other similar cases. I only beg you to take care that the members of the consistory remain unshaken, and do not suffer themselves to be alarmed by new rumours, calumnies, and threatenings. Moreover, let me know, through Boos, whether I should try to influence the bishop's mind, and to confirm him in his first conviction of the purity of Boos' doctrine and the blamelessness of his character.

" It is lamentable that scholastic and formal Christians will brand the inward leadings of God and the Divine life in Christ (which Paul says is 'hid with God') with the opprobrious epithets of mysticism and enthusiasm, by which pious minds are alarmed, and the weak are led astray. But the grace of God can discern and rescue innocence in the midst of calumnies, and truth in the midst of falsehoods.

" The Spirit of truth has enlightened you— the Spirit of power has strengthened you ; so that, recognising in the doctrine falsely called heretical, the ancient Catholic apostolic faith, you stand as a champion of the truth, and are not ashamed to be ranked by the other party among the deceived and misled. Verily, the gospel is so divine as to make us ready to bear any reproach for its sake ; and the peace of God is so precious, that we may well resign our worldly honours in order to gain it !"

Bertgen, in reply, urged Sailer to write to bishop Sigmund, to whom, accordingly, he addressed a forcible letter on August 15th.

Boos was thus favoured with some repose. But bishop Sigmund and the consistory gradually gave way to his enemies, and hesitated to pronounce too decidedly in favour of a man who was accused of heresy. The malcontents presented a new complaint, to the effect that Boos preached just in the same manner as before ; that he distributed prohibited books ; that he held intercourse, and kept up a correspondence, with Protestants ; and they had even the audacity to assert that he actually inflicted blows on persons who would not assent to his statements.

It was in vain that the consistory had declared that Boos was not a heretic ; he was held up as such by the neighbouring clergy. Thus the decision of the consistory was set at nought ; and the feeble protection which, for a time, it threw around Boos, was incapable of withstanding the new storm that was rising.

CHAPTER XV.

THE government having been informed of the unsettled state of things at Gallneukirch, appointed a commission of laymen and ecclesiastics to examine into the whole affair.

On the 3rd January, 1812, the commission arrived in great pomp, consisting of Von Bernberg, the president of the district, dean Huber, of Freystadt, and the secretary Schuh. The whole town was in commotion. The enemies of Boos made sure of the victory; while his friends put up fervent prayers to God for the triumph of the truth. The commissioners immediately summoned Boos before them. The following is his own account of the examination in a letter, dated January 12, 1812 :—

"What have you done up to the present time," they asked, "to reconcile your dissatisfied parishioners ?"

"I have called together those who were most opposed to me, and asked them what complaint they had to make against me. They replied, 'We have nothing ; only Brunner and Conrad say that you are a Lutheran.' I have explained my meaning in reference to the points that gave offence. I have prayed and wept for them ; I have sent some of their relations and friends to them in order to bring them to a better state of mind. At the confessional and in the pulpit I have endeavoured to make my sentiments intelligible; and lastly, I have written to them.'

" Have you strictly adhered to the directions of the bishop and the vicar-general ?"

" As much as possible ; but they have not forbidden me to preach living faith, and therefore I have continued to preach it. For woe be to me if, through the fear of man, I cease to preach the gospel !"

" Have you again preached 'living faith' in Jesus since the last warning of the consistory ?"

" Yes ; not to preach this I should consider to be a sin, for it is written, 'Whosoever is ashamed of me and of my words, of him will I be ashamed before my Father and his holy angels.'"

" Here," says Boos, " I began a long address, to which they all listened in silence ; I cannot now repeat what I said : but all present were much affected."

" Have you not," they asked, " shown the decision of the consistory to several persons ?"

" Certainly."

" Have you not said that you had gained

the cause, and that your accusers were obliged
to pay the costs ?"

" To the first part of this question I may
reply affirmatively, in a qualified sense ; to the
second part, with a direct negative."

" Are you not aware of the complaints
brought against you ?"

" Yes ; that I preach so much about living
faith—that I reject good works—and that I
am inclined to Lutheranism."

" Have you continued to preach about faith
since the last admonition ?"

" Yes."

" Did you not lately attack on purpose those
who were opposed to you ?"

" No."

" Do you not ascribe all evil and sickness
to Satan ?"

" To original sin, the evil principle, whether
called Satan or otherwise.   In the Holy Scriptures many diseases are ascribed to Satan.
Whether this or that disease be from Satan,
who can tell ?   I have only asserted in general,
that, as the Scriptures affirm, by the malice of
the devil and by sin, death, and all evil, come
into the world."

" There were other questions that I have
forgotten, to which I gave answers at length.
The questions and looks of the commissioners
do not please me.   To-day (the 4th) things
went rather better.   I was asked, How long
I had been in orders ?   Where ?   In what
capacity ?   How long minister at Postlinberg ?

How long here? Whether I have preached these principles in every place, or only here? Why they have produced disturbances only here? Why not in Suabia? Why I did not desist when I knew that my preaching created disturbances?"

In a second letter, dated January 7th and 12th, he thus writes:—

"I have now been scourged, that is, examined, for the fourth time, and tortured by many hundred unmeaning questions. The commissioners seem to be very much perplexed; they cannot yet tell where the fault lies. They do not believe in the existence of the devil. If one ventures to say a word about this liar and murderer, they laugh and sneer. Yesterday afternoon they examined, for the first time, the parochial authorities, who all spoke in my favour, and against Brunner. This had a good effect in diminishing the prejudices of the commissioners on the side of my accusers. They are now anxious to accommodate matters, and bring about a reconciliation. But the local judges are afraid that, in that case, the expenses of the commission would fall on them. Hence they will not render us assistance, unless they are certain of being free from loss. But I have this moment heard that the complainants will not enter into any accommodation. Twenty parish officers have just come from the sessions-house very indignant, saying that the malcontents were admitted while they were shut out. The dean

had told them that they might go home, for
the complainants would enter into no accommodation, and the decision must rest with the
government and the consistory. . . . At six
o'clock, Bernberg sent for me to the sessions-
house. On my arrival, he said, ' I am very
sorry that I have not been able to redeem my
promise, and effect a reconciliation between you
and your parishioners ; they wish to leave it
to the decision of the government. The commission is now closed. Everything will be left
in the hands of the supreme government and
the consistory. I entreat you not to provoke
the displeasure of your parishioners by offensive
expressions in the pulpit,' etc.

" We parted at last on tolerably good terms,
and knew as much after the commission as
before. Parties run as high as ever. There are
the same painful apprehensions and trials of
our faith. At the close of the proceedings, six
of the townsmen became sureties for me. The
commissioners afterwards went to practise
archery at the inn. The chaplains were in-
vited ; I remained, as usual, at home. Every
body around me is at their ease, but I am
stripped and hanging on the cross, and know
not when I shall be taken down. I have told
the commissioners that I am leading an uncom-
fortable life, and would gladly quit the place ;
but I will not leave of my own accord ; which
would be to act like a hireling. If my superiors
order me away, I shall consider it as God's
command. I shall shake the dust of this place

off my feet, and go first to Kirchberg—and then, I know not whither ; the world is large enough for Martin Boos. . . . . I am wonderfully humbled, exercised in the faith, and tried, and by this exercise I am strengthened, and my disciples with me.   We should be glad if this trial were over. But such is not the Lord's will ; we must continue in this school, that we may learn to know Christ better ; for we do not know him well enough yet."

In a letter to his friend, the Rev. Mr. Langenmeier, dated January 15, 1812, Boos says: " Grace and peace be with you from God ! From man there is neither grace nor peace !— I have just been with Bertgen and Herzog at Lintz ; they trembled like aspen-leaves, and despaired of my cause ; for, from all they can learn, the two commissioners, and all the rest, from the least to the greatest, are against me and the doctrine of the Lord. The following charges are brought against me :—

" 1. That I am connected with Catholics and Protestants in a secret society, which is strictly forbidden in Austria ; and the proof of this is, that I assumed the name *Zobo*. But what of this ? God knows that my fellowship is only with living believers, and my most secret friends are Sailer and yourself. Is it to be inferred that every intimate friendship constitutes a secret, unlawful society ? 2. That I wish to reform the whole Austrian clergy, or to bring them into disrepute by giving out that no one preaches Christ and his gospel but myself. But this is not to be tolerated. Therefore, away with the foreigner. 'Better that one should die, than that all should perish.' 3. My intercourse and correspondence with Theophilus and Höchstetter is a shocking thing in the eyes of the blind. 4. The Augsburg consistory has sent the whole investigation of 1797, with the fourteen propositions, to Lintz. Bernberg showed me them in a manuscript of ten sheets. With this they intend to refute entirely what Sailer has written against Huth and on my behalf, and to throw suspicion on Sailer himself. 5. My doctrine of justification savours to them of Protestantism, and leads, they assert, to an immoral life.

" From all this you may see that I am well nigh lost to Gallneukirch. My two friends, Bertgen and Herzog, tremble and shrink back; they scarcely dare venture to converse, still less to correspond, with me. . . . Three years ago I wished to leave this place, and might easily have gone ; but now, when I have so many believing children, and when such a step must be attended with shame and disgrace, it is exceedingly painful. . . . Disturbances may still occur in my parish. The well-disposed say, If our minister were on the bridge across the Danube, on his way to leave us, we would all stand on the bridge, and pull him back again to Gallneukirch. One party would drive me out of the country, and another would keep me in it. Advise me what to do in these perplexing circumstances. Am I to ask for my dismission, or to persevere? I prefer the latter. 'The hireling fleeth ; the good shepherd giveth his life for the sheep.' I will go only if God removes me by means of the government."

Six months after the commissioners had discharged their office, the following mandate was issued by the consistory, dated July 1, 1812:—

"The rev. Martin Boos is most seriously admonished by the consistory to be totally silent respecting faith, justification, and other points, which were brought forward in the last investigation ;—or, if it should be unavoidably necessary to speak on such subjects, either in preaching, or at the confessional, or in private instruction or conversation, he must make use of no other expressions than those employed by the rest of the Catholic clergy, according to the symbolical books."

This injunction reminded Boos of that of the high priests to the apostles, to "speak to no man henceforth in the name of Jesus;" and the reply of the apostles on that occasion would correctly express his own sentiments respecting it : "Whether it be right in the sight of God to hearken unto you more than unto God, judge ye. For we cannot but speak the things which we have seen and heard." (Acts iv. 17—20.)

On the very day that the mandate of the consistory was issued, Boos lost his faithful friend and advocate, Bertgen, who died after a short illness, in his fifty-first year. "His death," said Boos, "has renewed all my

sorrows. My enemies rejoice, and assume a
higher tone. But when I think of my departed
friend, I am led to admire more than ever the
glorious power of God, should he be pleased to
rescue me from the hands of my enemies. But
should he suffer me to fall before them, he will
be the same glorious Lord as in past ages, and I
shall be the same poor sinner as I have ever
been. It is our lot to decrease. Be not offended
at that; where and when has the world acknowledged and honoured real saints? How
can we expect it? It neither sees nor knows
us. Are the servants greater than their
Lord?"

In the midst of these severe trials, Boos was
not left without those marks of the Divine
approbation which a faithful servant of Christ
prizes beyond all others, namely, the success of
his ministry in converting men to God. A remarkable instance of this occurred in reference
to a person who had been one of his bitterest
opponents. Boos gives the following account
in a letter to a friend :—

"One of my chief adversaries had a child
born yesterday, which died in the course of the
night. At eight this morning he came and
asked me, in a very respectful manner, to bury
it. My heart beat faster when I heard his
voice, for I knew him to be an enemy, and I
hesitated whether I should enter into conversation with him or not. Taking courage, however, I said, ' My good friend, how are you in
other respects? Can you not yet be cordial

with me ?' He appeared surprised and confused, and knew not what to say. So I began again, 'The superintendent of the district told me that you were the most considerable of all my opponents, and that he knew for certain, that you would very shortly come and be reconciled with me. I have now waited almost a year, and have seen nothing of you. How is this ?'

" ' Oh ! it is a bad business ; I would give a good deal to be out of it.'

" ' You may very easily get out of it.'

" ' How, pray ?'

" ' Believe in Jesus Christ, as I and others do; so will you be out of it, and be saved.'

" ' You are always saying we ought to believe —we do that already.'

" ' There, my friend, you are mistaken ; you have *not* done that already. People may say with the lips that they believe; but the heart is far from it. As it is in prayer, so it is in believing. If living faith were not deficient, the Catholic church would not always pray, ' Lord, increase our faith.' She would not every Sunday excite faith, hope, and love, if it were not necessary, and if she did not know that these graces may languish at any time, and expire.'

" ' Very true.'

" ' Observe, Christ did signs and wonders, and yet they believed not, or only for a season : how often he reproached his disciples for being so slow to believe !'

" ' But there has never been a clergyman here who has preached so much about faith, and made it of so much importance, as you have done.'

" ' You have given me occasion to do so.'

" ' How so ?'

" ' Because one of your number hung himself, owing to unbelief, and many of you were half in despair. I then saw that the foundation, the basis of human salvation, was not yet laid. Therefore I thought it necessary to begin with this people from the very beginning—to lay the foundation-stone, Christ, and then build upon that the gold, silver, and precious stones of good works; or, in other words, to plant first in you the good tree, Christ, in order that from the good tree, good fruit may be brought, since unless Christ be in us, we can do nothing good.'

" ' But you make getting to heaven such an easy matter ; and yet it is said that we cannot enter it without earnest striving.'

" ' Yes ; it requires such earnest striving, that up to this time you have not taken the first step, which is to believe in Christ. You have not yet fulfilled this which is the first command. Do you not perceive that it is difficult, very difficult, to believe ?'

" ' Yes, it is so, indeed !'

" ' But as soon as we believe, everything becomes easy. Christ himself says, ' My yoke is easy, and my burden is light,' Matt. xi. 29. And he compares the kingdom of heaven to a marriage feast, where all things are ready, and nothing is necessary, but to come to it. Christ therefore makes it easy.   Shall I make it harder ?'

" ' I am exceedingly glad,' he replied, ' that you have conversed on this subject, and given me such information.   I will now tell you how I came to take part in this affair.   I had read Henke and Huth, and I asked father Conrad whether a church history could say what was false.   ' No,' he answered; ' it is equal to the Catholic church, under whose inspection alone it can be published.'   So also said Brunner; I believed him, and thus have been led into perplexity.   But now I perceive that lies may appear in print.   Allow me to call upon you frequently; it will end, I am sure, in our being of one heart and one mind.'

" ' Come, whenever you please.'

" ' I was most excited by the Bavarian clergyman who told us in his sermon that we were seduced by the devil.   In our anger, we were ready to tear him and you in pieces, and only wanted a good opportunity.' "

Boos then read various passages of Scripture to him: on which he remarked, "I have often told my wife and friends that St. Paul writes quite in favour of our pastor's views, but St. James is against him."

"James is not against me," said Boos ; "he speaks of the righteousness which avails before men, and of sanctification, which I do not reject. Go and do as many good works as you please ; I will not prevent you."

They conversed together for two hours longer, with mutual satisfaction. At length Boos said, " I entreat you to try faith in Christ for a quarter of a year. How many have tried gluttony, drunkenness, and lewdness, for a much longer period !" He replied, " I will try it."

" Yes ; try it ; it is God's first command— the first article in the catechism: you cannot be doing wrong."

CHAPTER XVI.

The imperial mandate—Boos during the war of 1812.—Letter of Anna Schlatter.

THE commissioners made their report to the supreme government. But before the latter had come to a decision, the adversaries of Boos used their utmost efforts to prejudice the court against him, as a dangerous man who taught doctrines that tended to lead the people into error.

The imperial mandate was dated Nov. 19, 1812; though not formally communicated to Boos till the end of the following January. The substance of it is as follows:—

"The minister of Gallneukirch, judging from some of his discourses, is a person strongly disposed to mysticism, and imprudent in his expressions, but not a heretic.

"From the documentary evidence it appears that, out of a population of four thousand souls, only two priests and thirty of his parishioners have taken offence at some of his views and statements. Yet his injudicious and partial representation of the doctrine of justification, tending more to enthusiasm than to the practical performance of duty, in the constant announcement of which he persists, to the neglect of the useful lessons of practical Christianity, cannot be approved.

" Owing to the uncommonly strong attachment of the greater part of the congregation to his person, and the blamelessness of his general conduct, and in the absence of other evidence against him, nothing can be decided as to his immediate removal from his parish ; gentler means must first be tried . . . . . The bishop's court will endeavour to correct his mystical views by direct instruction; by the inspection of his sermons before they are delivered; and by appointing him an able co-adjutor. The same court will also take care that the neighbouring clergy do nothing that may disturb the peace of his congregation. Should these measures not correct his errors and restore peace to the parish, his removal to another will be indispensable, and even his dismissal from the pastoral office, should he persist in his enthusiastic notions, and in promulgating his one-sided doctrines in spite of all persecution, as he calls it. But as to the charge of uttering disloyal sentiments, it has no better foundation than the idle gossip of a woman, which was not thought worth taking down, and the deposition of a man who seems to have totally misunderstood the drift of his language."

When Boos appeared before the consistory this decision of the supreme court was communicated to him; but in a very garbled manner, with the omission of those passages that were most in his favour.

The members of the consistory had been directed to point out what they considered injudicious, partial, or enthusiastic, in his statements. But instead of doing so, they satisfied themselves with vaguely enjoining upon him to preach like the other clergy in the diocese, and requiring him to submit his sermons to inspection before they were delivered.

Such were the painful circumstances in which Boos was now placed. His parishioners, amounting to four or five thousand souls, besides many persons from a distance, had been delighted and edified by his discourses; many had been converted to God, and built up in the faith; yet he was now to sit as a scholar at the feet of preachers who often did not believe what they preached, nor preach what they believed. And men destitute of living faith themselves were not likely to instruct him to preach in a manner that would awaken others.

" Although the emperor," said Boos, in one of his letters, " has acquitted me, yet I am not certain for a single day, that I shall not be superseded, or altogether ejected from the clerical office, since hell and the world are incessantly assailing me. But let them go on; so must I; the Almighty can still hold me up. The extraordinary attachment of my parishioners has, at this time, enabled me to keep my post. Otherwise it would have been all over with such a feeble old man as myself. My enemies would have devoured me, in order to feast on my parish. Gruber said he suspected that envy was secretly at work. He saw and spoke the truth. .... On the 28th of July I was again cited before the consistory, and signed five propositions, which were laid before me, and which, after some brief explanations, I acknowledged to be true. I scarcely think that I shall live to the end of this contest. .... On August 20th, I was struck with paralysis on the whole of my right side, so that I could not write a single letter. But, through God's mercy and medical aid, I am so far recovered, that I am just able to scrawl these lines. I had rest externally, when the Lord was thus pleased to afflict me in my own person, that I might never be without a cross. .... The result of my process, and the four examinations that so rapidly succeeded each other, is still undecided, and the world therefore cannot tell whether its prince or Christ has gained the victory. Meanwhile, there is a perfect calm, just as if nothing whatever had happened. In these last attacks I have suffered, till I am weary of life. My enemies have taken notes of my sermons, and laid copies of them before the consistory, which I am required to revise, and write the corrections in the margin. They have also sent to the consistory sheets full of what I have uttered at the confessional or in my pastoral visits. All these attacks I have had to rebut. The accusations of my adversaries with my answers are now gone to Vienna. ... "W. calls the few propositions which the consistory laid before me a compendium of the gospel. I never expected any thing so unexceptionable from that quarter. ... Christ crucified forms their basis, so that we are satisfied with them. I have already publicly lectured on them, and given them to my parishioners to copy."

Germany was, at this time, the seat of war. The victories of the French armies had spread universal desolation in that country. At such a crisis, Boos and his friends had an opportunity of exhibiting the practical effect of the truths for holding which they had been so abused and calumniated. He made a public collection for the wounded soldiers, and so liberal were the contributions, that he received the cordial thanks of the very men who had accused him of depreciating good works.

After having been incessantly harassed for about three years, Boos enjoyed a twelvemonth's quiet; but on September 20, 1814, a severe injunction was forwarded to him from Vienna and from Lintz, to the following effect :—

"That the doctrine of justification is a speculative subject, and on that account not adapted for popular discourses. That Boos ought to present religion in a practical point of view. That his zealous endeavours to lower human pride and to excite humble gratitude for God's grace would be much more successful, if he would exhort men to the practice of what is good, and then show that we must also regard our good works as the gift of God. That, generally speaking, he had not corrected several errors which he had before committed in the discharge of his pastoral office, as, for instance, in distributing Bibles, and an enthusiastic work entitled " The Book of the Heart." That his manner of treating the doctrine of Divine grace was palpably one-sided. That as to the doctrine of justification, he must conform most strictly to the directions of the consistory and adhere to the phraseology they recommend. In case of non-compliance, he would be forthwith removed from the parish. That it seemed advisable that he should, if possible, obtain another appointment." The consistory of Lintz added, " That if pastor Boos did not punctually and invariably conform to these instructions, steps would be immediately taken to remove him from his living."

As might have been expected, Boos would not comply with these injunctions. He had already referred his cause to a higher authority than that of any ecclesiastical court whatever, even that of Jesus Christ, from whom he had received his commission. He continued, therefore, to preach in the same style as he had been wont. At length the emperor Francis, weary of the whole affair with which he had been so long annoyed, and convinced of the injustice and malevolence of the complainants, imposed on them absolute silence, under pain of severe punishment.

" All around me are exulting," Boos wrote, at the beginning of December, " and congratulating me on having gained the victory; since it is now ascertained that the emperor has silenced and punished my adversaries. It has come out, that they have been in the practice, for three or four years past, of taking down my sermons *verbatim*, and forwarding copies of them to the emperor, in order to prove that I was a heretic and an enthusiast. The emperor, who knew of the proceedings against me since the year 1811, laid them before the Vienna consistory, and, when nothing objectionable was found in the discourses, ordered these court-scribes to be severely reprimanded and punished."

But this second season of repose was not of long duration. The 24th of July, 1815, was the last day spent by Boos at Gallneukirch, for on that day he was summoned before the consistory at Lintz. Of the proceedings on this occasion, he gives the following account in a letter to his friend, Anna Schlatter:—

" On the 23rd of July, late in the evening, a special messenger came to Gallneukirch with an order from the bishop's court for me to appear before the consistory at nine o'clock the next morning. On the 24th, accordingly, Zobo stood before the council, the bishop and all the other members of it were present—nine huntsmen and one hare! Your letters and those of all the brethren were publicly read, misconstrued, ridiculed, and vilified, till my heart bled. This lasted for six hours. I defended myself and you as far as ability was given me, but all to no purpose. After being told to withdraw, I was again called in, when the bishop pronounced the following sentence :— 'I hereby deprive you of all clerical authority. I allow you to remain no longer in your living, nor in my diocese, nor in this country. All the counsellors here assembled unite in this decision. You will therefore remain here, dine with me at noon, and then go to the prison at the Carmelite convent, to await there the emperor's final sentence. It appears from these letters that you are a leading member of a secret pietest society, and the emperor does not allow such in his dominions.'

"I have now been five weeks in confinement, though, on the 22nd, its severity was so far relaxed, that I was allowed to go into the city. The prophet has now his cell, his wooden stool, his candlestick, and his bed, (2 Kings iv. 10.) And there he awaits the emperor's final sentence. No human being—God alone is with him, and gives him abundant consolation. Let us rejoice and be glad in the Lord, and trust in him."

In another letter he says :—" Three persons occasionally visit me: the bishop, who always quarrels with me, my keeper, and professor Ziegler ; the two latter sympathise and make kind inquiries. But not a word is allowed to pass between me and my parishioners, who often stand before my cell with weeping eyes. Ought we not to go among the heathen, since Christians will not allow the gospel to have free course ? . . . Many letters have never reached us, but have fallen into the hands of spies. . . . The magistrates found us guilty of no offence, either political or religious, but only of being living saints and (in their opinion) righteous overmuch ; but the consistory discovered many sins, particularly that mortal and capital one, a secret pietist society. You may perhaps learn from your friends what they will find us guilty of at Vienna."

Anna Schlatter, a Protestant lady in Switzerland, having been informed that the correspondence of Boos had been seized, and that one of the principal charges against him was the friendly intercourse he maintained with Protestants, wrote the following letter (before she heard of his imprisonment) to the canon Waldhauser, to explain how she became acquainted with Boos, and, if possible, to present his conduct in a more favourable light :—

" Saint Gall, Aug. 1, 1815.

" Love for the truth, and friendship for the venerable pastor Boos, give me courage to address these lines to you. Some weeks ago, I heard from several friends that the correspondence of our friend Boos had been examined, and I suspected that of the whole number, my letters would give the greatest offence. For this reason I am anxious to say a few words to you on the occasion of that correspondence, and also on the letters themselves. Only by a believing regard to Him who rewards every good deed done for his sake, and helps to bear all sufferings, can I endure the thought that the excellent Boos should be subjected to anything painful on account of me or my son.

"As to the circumstances that led to our correspondence, they were simply these. My son was employed as an artisan at Munich, and in one of his letters said that he wished to go to Vienna, and requested me to furnish him, if possible, with a letter of introduction to some one on the road. In Vienna itself I had a friend of some respectability, but on the way thither I knew no one. Now, for several years, I had been in the habit of hearing, through my friends, of the life and character of the minister of Gallneukirch, though I had had no personal or written communication with him. Remembering the admonition of our Lord and Saviour Jesus Christ, 'All things whatsoever ye would that men should do unto you, do ye also to them,' I have considered it my duty to afford to Catholics as well as Protestants, advice, personal aid, and sympathy, whenever I could, without asking, To which church do you belong?—my only questions have been, What do you need? and, Can I be of any service? According to this my own rule, I measured a far more advanced Christian, that man full of faith, Martin Boos; and wrote in confidence a letter of introduction to him for my son, in 1814, the first I ever wrote to him. The event proved that I was not deceived in my hopes, which were founded entirely on the principles of the gospel. It pleased God that as my son was crossing the river Isar, the bridge broke down; he and his luggage were saved, and, after a journey of some hours, he was glad to find in the excellent Boos all the aid that friendly care could give him. The manner in which this worthy disciple of Christ acted the part of the good Samaritan I can never forget till my heart ceases to beat. He was a father and a benefactor to my son, both for body and soul. Of course, my son sent me an account of these events; and Boos himself was so obliging as to inform me of my son's arrival and departure. How could any one with a mother's heart keep silence? You will imagine that a mother would bless, and ardently esteem, the benefactor of her child, even were he a Turk or a negro.

" Thus began the correspondence between the pastor Boos and a Protestant female. It is evident that my letters were addressed entirely from my heart to his heart, under the eye of God. Born and brought up in a land of

liberty, and in a church where compulsion of
conscience or examination of correspondence is
entirely unknown, I had no idea that my
letters would fall into any other hands than
those of my fatherly friend. Hence I wrote
many things which, but on this supposition, I
should never have penned. But as, according
to the words of Jesus, not a hair of my head
falls without the will of my heavenly Father,
so no letter of mine can come into any other
hands than those he pleases. Therefore, I do
not trouble myself. I only consider it a sacred
duty most humbly to request, that, in reference
to anything whatever objectionable in my
letters, not the shadow of an imputation may
rest upon beloved Boos, but altogether on myself. His letters to me have been always very
brief,—a few short sentences ; and I have given
him in return, woman-like, answers spun out
to a great length. I would gladly have been
instructed by him, and receive light on the
truths of the gospel from him. I still cherish
the hope that the times are approaching when
it will no more be asked, Are you of Paul? or
of Apollos ? but merely, Are you of Christ ?
when we shall all rejoice together in one
common confession of faith, which is daily
repeated by many members of all the three
churches, ' I believe in one holy, Catholic,
Christian church, the communion of saints,'
etc. Will you charge Boos with holding
erroneous sentiments on account of my private
views, which I press on no one ?

"Should you consider it necessary for the comfort of this man of God and his congregation, I will not write to him again as long as he is at Gallneukirch. Although his letters, so full of unction, are very edifying to me, his humility brings down my proud self-righteousness, and his confidence in the power and spirit of Christ has raised my courage in the conflict against sin, yet I will gladly make the sacrifice for his comfort; for the Spirit of Christ does not depend on man. Christ alone is perfect. Men are all frail, as Paul, John, and James themselves testify.

"Meanwhile, I believe that my views, which (according to the measure of knowledge given to such a weak individual) have been drawn from God's word, and make me cheerful, peaceful, and active in my own circle, would have injured no one, as far as I have communicated them, had they been left in my friend's desk. That they have been brought forth and examined, and thus become a subject of debate and public animadversion, is not our fault; and was, indeed, against our will. But of old, controversy has been the most powerful means of diffusing the controverted points among the people. Where, on the contrary, toleration and quiet have existed, the people have continued in their ancient faith. Boos would not have had so many followers if he had always been left alone.

"May our Lord Jesus Christ, who shed his blood for the life of the world, be pleased to kindle faith in him, and love to him, in all hearts, that the earth may be full of his praise and glory.   That his grace may be with you, is the prayer of your most humble servant,

" ANNA SCHLATTER, formerly BERNET."

CHAPTER XVII.

Boos in confinement at Lintz.

DURING his confinement in the monastery at Lintz, Boos received much kindness from two officers who, though not pious men, were indignant at the treatment he had received, and obtained permission to visit him. But his keepers soon deprived him of this solace, and made his confinement absolutely solitary. Two young monks, however, who felt grateful to him for his spiritual instructions, earnestly desired to lighten, if possible, the pressure of his captivity. Being denied all direct personal intercourse with him, they had recourse to an ingenious contrivance which enabled him to communicate with his friends. One day Boos observed something coming down from the story above his cell. At first he could not tell what it was, but on opening his casement found it was a roasted turkey fastened to a string. He immediately guessed that it was let down by some friendly hand, and took it in. But what was his joy to find, carefully concealed in the fowl, pens, ink, and paper! He soon concluded who were his generous and ingenious benefactors.

More than once they adopted this method of communication; the same string carried back his letters, which his trusty friends forwarded according to their address.

Thus Boos kept up a correspondence with his brethren for several months. But he discovered a still simpler method. Having noticed in his apartment a small hole in the wall made by the mice, through which they passed and repassed every day, the thought struck him that he could transmit his letters through the same aperture. His friends, taking advantage of the time when no one was in the passage, forwarded their answers in the same way. But to avoid detection, it was necessary to be very cautious. He could only write at night, by the feeble glimmer of a lamp; when he hastily committed to paper words full of life and energy, to revive the drooping spirits of his anxious friends. His inkstand was placed under his bed, and if the least noise reached his ear he at once concealed his pen and paper under the mattrass. It was by this means that he wrote the following letter to Anna Schlatter:—

"Lintz, Sept. 1815.— . . . The bishop has read your letters with pleasure. See! a wide field is before you, to open eyes which have never yet beheld the pure light of the gospel. They treat our awakenings as illusions, self-deception, womanish fancies, and yet they will hold communication with you who alone have found favour in their eyes. Show them that you, and all of us, are not imposed upon, are not deceived and dazzled by our faith in Christ. Point them to a Mary, an Elizabeth, a Hannah, a Magdalene, the Samaritan woman, the women at the grave of Jesus, Lydia, and others. Show them that ' God hath chosen the weak things of the world to confound them that are mighty,' that he often first trusted his secrets to women, and that the eleven apostles were upbraided for their unbelief and hardness of heart because they believed not the women. (Mark xvi. 14.) Show them that our friendship is no secret, revolutionary, or dangerous society."

"I thank you with tears," (he says, in another letter to the same friend,) "for the affection you manifest in expressing your readiness to receive me under your roof. I will wait till the emperor has examined my cause, and either approved or disapproved of it. I should grievously wound and offend my faithful flock, if I did not wait for the decision of the emperor, whom they have petitioned in my behalf. I would rather die in prison than vex or grieve my brethren. But if I am condemned, I will request you and yours to receive me as an exile. I would not lead an idle life, and subsist on charity, but labour, and eat what I gain by my labour. Now I am doing nothing, and for eight weeks have tasted the sweets of idleness! I have been eighteen years in Austria, and have acquired the right of citizenship; but I am unwilling to remain where I should perhaps be unemployed, or live and die under constant inspection, like a slave. I thank your sister for her kind sympathy. But the cross must first be borne. The present is not the time to think of rest. When the measure of my sufferings is full, then God will deliver me, and grant me rest, either in the grave, or with you."

To another friend (Jungson) he thus writes: "October 2, 1815.—You have probably heard that since the 24th of July, after seizing all my correspondence, and examining me for six hours, they have confined me in the prison of the convent, where I am awaiting the emperor's final decision. You must not disturb yourself on my account; for what has happened to me to-day in the east, may be your own lot to-morrow in the west; if you continue to believe and to labour. . . . . It is almost incredible that a doctrine so holy and productive of happiness should not be tolerated in the midst of Christendom. But so it is. How, otherwise, here, in the heart of Christendom, should I be confined for ten weeks in a cold prison; and formerly, at Augsburg, for a year and a half. My brother! it is a fact; the devil even now, casts some into prison. (Rev. ii. 10.) We must, like the primitive disciples, be willing to forsake house and lands for Christ's sake. . . . . It is a clear mark of our brotherhood in Christ that we endure the same sufferings and enjoy the same blessings. Therefore, like Peter and Paul, let us give one another the right hand of fellowship. . . . . I entreat you to grant me your fervent prayers; for my faith and yours are vehemently assailed in all

quarters, not excepting the imperial court.
Everywhere we are looked upon as sectarians,
mystics, hypocrites, and members of secret
societies. And who are the persons that say
these things? Those who are regarded as the
most pious and intelligent. So that oftentimes
I can only weep and pray. Pray for me, that
my smoking flax may not be quenched!"

Some alleviation of the rigour of his confinement was afforded Boos by a person who, from
his situation in life, might have been expected
to show little sympathy for such a prisoner.
In the garrison of Lintz was an officer who had
been one of his catechumens at Unterthingau
in 1790. This brave soldier had never forgotten the pious instructions of his pastor, and the
affectionate interest he had taken in his welfare,
six-and-twenty years before. No sooner did
he hear of Boos's confinement than he hastened
to the monastery, and requested permission to
see him. On being admitted, he threw himself into the good man's arms, who at first had
some difficulty in recalling him to mind, but
on recognising him pressed him to his heart
with joy. The captain offered him all the
service in his power. But what could he do
for a man under close confinement? Let Boos
tell us in his own words.

" . . . . The captain, who was once my
pupil, is more to me in prison than Lysias and
Julius were to Paul; he sends his servant three
times a day to me. He is not yet a believer,

but weeps whenever he receives letters from me. God grant that he and his wife may obtain mercy, as he (like Onesiphorus) has showed mercy to me!"

This officer wrote to one of his friends (June 26, 1816) as follows:—" We are full of grief, I and my family, on account of the sufferings of my former teacher, Martin Boos, whose character is all love and goodness. I remember how often in my childhood he dried up my tears, when he was curate at Unterthingau, and with what unwearied benevolence he attended the sick, night and day. I call to mind with what earnestness and warmth he imparted his instructions; and how zealously he fulfilled his ministry. I often think of the day when, having performed the last offices for my dear father, Boos gave me his last piece of money and encouraged me to redouble my application to my studies." The captain never forgot the poor curate's generosity. Whenever Boos begged him not to lavish so much attention upon him, the grateful soldier stopped him by saying, " You gave me your last coin."

Boos to Anna Schlatter.

" 24 Nov. 1815.—Our good captain begged the bishop to let me dine with him on St. Martin's day. The prelate having consented, I breathed the pure fresh air for the first time again since I came hither. I had only five hundred paces to go, and yet perspired as if I had walked as many leagues. After being so long immured, the fresh air was too much for me. . . . I bless God that, on the whole, I have been preserved in health, which I ascribe to the prayers of yourself and all my other friends. Since the 24th of July, it is true, my hours have not always been of the same·character in this solitary confinement ; some have been burning, and melting, like fire ; others happy and cheerful as heaven. Yes, I am a sinner, and eternal love finds enough in me to burn, to pull down, to polish, to correct. The consolation contained in Rom. viii. 1, has often forsaken me when I only saw my sins, and my desert of eternal condemnation; and I could scarcely believe what I preached to others. Very often I could not say with St. Paul, 'I am persuaded that neither death, nor life, nor angels, nor principalities, nor powers, nor things present, nor things to come, nor height, nor depth, nor any other creature, shall be able to separate us from the love of God which is in Christ Jesus our Lord.' For I saw in and about myself nothing but defilement, chains, and bonds ; and then all assurance of salvation vanished. But so much the more must I again lay hold of the Saviour as my only refuge. You have read my heart and seen all that passes there. But Satan has not only painted my sins in the blackest colours before my eyes, but has also represented the good that proceeds from grace and faith, as evil; and thus I have been smitten within and without, and on all sides. I experienced

similar trials, and chastisement, in my first
imprisonment in 1797, but it seemed as new
to me now, as if I had never known it before. I have made use of it as you advised;
I have examined my heart and life; I have
confessed my sins before the Lord, and besought
him weeping; and he has quieted my heart,
and taken away my sins."

"I am not so unhappy," (says Boos, in
another letter,) "as they imagine; for 'the kingdom of heaven'—real joy, true satisfaction—is
'within us.' Hence I often enjoy more happiness amidst reproaches and bonds than when
free from them, since I now keep the one thing
needful more constantly in my eye. We esteem the blood and righteousness of Christ as
our ornament and glorious apparel : but to
prevent the perversion and abuse of faith, we
add, Live as piously and holily as if you were
to be justified and saved by your own piety
and imperfect holiness; but withal, believe and
die as those who are alone justified and saved
through the merits of Christ. Thus we unite
Paul's justification by faith (Rom. iii. 24) with
James's justification by works (ii. 14, 20.) The
best and most pious man cannot support himself
on his own virtue and holiness, (Gal. iii. 10,)
either in life or in death."

CHAPTER XVIII.

Petition of the parish of Gallneukirch to the emperor of Austria —Letter from Boos to the archbishop of Vienna.

NEARLY two months had elapsed since the day Boos entered the convent of the Carmelites as a prisoner. His parishioners deeply resented this act as decidedly unjust. With the exception of a few individuals, whose hostility was fostered by some priests in the neighbourhood, the mass of the population, consisting of four thousand souls and upwards, were filled with sorrow at the proceedings against their minister. More than once they had protested against the intolerance of his enemies, but without effect. At last, hoping that the emperor would be more favourably disposed, they drew up and presented the following petition :—

"May it please your majesty,—The parish of Gallneukirch has suffered poignant sorrow on account of their honoured pastor, Boos, with whom they have been satisfied for so many years, during which time he has been their confessor, instructor, and comforter,— that, without any known, adequate cause, he has been removed, imprisoned, and deprived of all clerical authority. It is now more than six weeks that he has been confined in the convent of the Carmelites at Lintz. And though his parishioners have respectfully and sorrowfully requested, both in writing and verbally, of the bishop and the civil authorities, to inform them of the grounds of this harsh procedure, and to comfort them in their sufferings and distress by an explanation of the circumstances ; yet, in spite of all their efforts, they can gain nothing; and their painful state of ignorance is aggravated by the apparent inconsistency of his judges, since the venerable consistory itself declares, ' That the pastor Boos has not been guilty of any moral or political delinquency, but merely wishes to lead a hidden, inward life with God and Christ.'

" That the pastor Boos cannot have done anything contrary to your majesty's wish and command, or that his course of life (founded on a good conscience and a loving trust in God and his holy Son) could be displeasing to your majesty, his parishioners, amounting at least to four thousand, cannot believe. Hence they humbly request your majesty and the supreme court to restore the pastor Boos to his bereaved and forlorn parish—to cut short, or, at least, to lighten his confinement, and to expedite the termination of the proceedings against him.

" The parishioners are ready to pledge themselves that neither the state nor the church has anything to fear from this individual. For nine years they have personally witnessed the patriotic sentiments which animate him. During that period, he has borne every public and private burden with unexampled patience and promptitude. He has furnished supplies, quarters, and relays, and everything else, often beyond his means, and without being required to do so. He has exhorted them to obedience to the monarch and government, and to voluntary contributions for the sick and wounded soldiers. His conduct has been blameless ; and his doctrine purely Catholic and scriptural. The whole parish is perfectly satisfied and contented. But the neighbouring clergy are always envying and persecuting him, because they consider themselves slighted and injured by his good example and doctrine. Hence, disunion has been introduced into our parochial meetings; and the principle is attempted to be established that he is a foreigner, and ought not to have the living. It is lamentable that so excellent a clergyman, now sixty years old, and moreover sickly and infirm, and who has worn himself out by his incessant labours, should be persecuted as if he were a notorious offender, and with a severity which will soon exhaust him, both in body and soul, unless your majesty vouchsafe to show him favour and compassion.

" The parish wishes for no other pastor, and humbly prays for his continuance. All impartial clergymen and ecclesiastics, as well as all the people, can see no cause why this pious, able, and intelligent man should be deprived of his honours and jurisdiction, his spiritual power and office, and of his very health ; or perhaps left destitute in his old age, and forced to leave the country when helpless and infirm.

"Your majesty, on September 20, 1812, received a deputation in favour of Mr. Boos, and was pleased to determine that justice should be done him, and that his calumniators should be punished according to law. Yet this punishment has never been inflicted ; and hence so much uneasiness still exists on this subject, and disturbances are kept up by malicious and slanderous men. We call to mind with tears the paternal expressions of your majesty, ' If you, my children, are girt about with truth and righteousness (as you say) you will be assisted by truth and righteousness ; and both you and your pastor may at all times come to me, and find protection.' These gracious words we shall never forget ; and hence our dejected and persecuted parish appeals to your majesty's sense of justice, and to the righteous decision of the supreme court. . . . The parish request that at least the pastor Boos may be sent for to Vienna, that he may there defend himself in person, and undergo a judicial examination, exempt from party feeling and envy."

Boos, on his part, in order to exculpate himself more completely from the charge of belonging to a secret society, obtained permission to address a letter to the archbishop of Vienna, in which he gives an account of his various correspondents both at home and abroad.

He begins with remarking, that as Fenelon, in his time, wrote to persons of all classes and conditions, men and women, old and young, healthy and sick, nobles and beggars, when they had recourse to him for advice and consolation, under their doubts and difficulties, respecting the way of salvation, so he had adopted a similar plan, without apprehending that he should be exposed to the charge of sinister views and illegal projects.

" My first and most distinguished correspondent," he goes on to say, "is MICHAEL SAILER, professor of moral and pastoral theology in Landshut. With him I have corresponded above thirty years. I attended his lectures in the University of Dillingen. He then gained my entire heart and confidence, as was the case with most of his pupils. When separated from him, and employed in ministerial duties, I applied to him as a young priest for counsel and information in all difficult cases ; as almost all did who had been under his care, for he refused none. I have continued to do the same during my residence in Austria ; and, so far from making a secret of it, I have done it with the knowledge of dean Bertgen and bishop Gall, and have shown them his answers, as they were readers and admirers of his writings. He has been their guest during the vacations, and travelled with them to Gallneukirch and Vienna.

Yet no one has charged them with maintaining a secret correspondence, or with being members of a secret pietist society.

"The second of my foreign correspondents was the late MICHAEL FENEBURG, minister in Seeg and Vaehringen. He was my fellow-countryman, relative, and friend,—was, like myself, subjected to examination at Augsburg, and he was in 1797 my vicar, whom I served as curate for two years merely for my board, after the amputation of his right leg. (See his Life, by Sailer, published at Munich in 1814.) When I afterwards removed into Austria, to attend to pastoral duties under the late bishop Gall, nothing could be more likely than that, united as we were by natural and spiritual ties, and by similar trials, we should correspond, and inform ourselves of each other's welfare; and 'since Feneburg was full of piety and faith in Christ, it was also to be expected that he should make mention of this faith in his letters. But it was never imagined that the commencement and continuance of this correspondence involved any secret association.

"My third correspondent was PRESIDENT VON RUOSH. I first became acquainted with this eminent priest, and still more eminent Christian, in the year 1790, when I was curate at Seeg; to which place he and his son came on a visit to my vicar Feneburg. In consequence of his staying some days at Seeg, and being of the same mind and religious spirit with his old friends Sailer and Feneburg, he and I became friends for the Lord's sake; and since he left his only son, Alois Ruosh, with us, for further instruction and education, in which we (that is, Feneburg, Bayer, and I) all took a part—a correspondence ensued as a matter of course. And as Ruosh was, and still is, a man of great piety, the letters with which he now and then favoured me, even after I settled in Austria, bore the stamp of his character. But neither Ruosh nor I ever dreamt of a secret, revolutionary association.

"The fourth was XAVER BAYR, at present minister in D. The origin of our friendship and correspondence was simply this:—We were fellow-students at Dillingen, under Sailer; we lived, laboured, and suffered together for two years as curates at Seeg; we were both subjected to the examination at Augsburg in 1797 (as may be seen in Sailer's Life of Feneburg;) we had the same dwelling, fare, labours, sufferings, mind, spirit, faith, hope, and love. What, therefore, could be more natural than that, after I was settled in Austria, and he at Algau in Suabia, we should write to one another?

"My fifth foreign correspondent was JOHN GOSSNER, formerly pastor in Munich. He also was my fellow-student at Dillingen, and a curate at Seeg with Feneburg; he was my companion in tribulation at Augsburg. Similar sufferings and fortunes made us friends. He likewise, after I had settled in Austria, inquired by letter respecting my circumstances, whether pleasant or painful. Having written several small religious works, he sent some of them to me, from a regard to our early friendship, and requested my opinion of them. This circumstance gave a religious turn to our correspondence : but no one could infer that our friendship was a secret association.

" The sixth is JOHN LANGENMAIER, formerly minister and school visitor in Kirchberg, near B., but now assistant preacher in G. He also studied with me at Dillingen; and as bishop's chaplain, was my comforter for nearly two years during the examination at Augsburg. He acted for me in receiving some property and a library which I inherited from my deceased uncle, counsellor Koegel. He received everything and disposed of what I could not take into Austria. In this instance also, it was very natural, and even necessary, for us to correspond on both temporal and spiritual affairs. Of the connexions he formed at a later period I knew nothing for several years, and when he laid them before me, in his letters, as matters of conscience, I was more alarmed than himself. But what was I to do with this sinner, as he was esteemed ? I could not easily dissolve r..y connexion with him, for, 1st, He had shown me many civilities at Augsburg, both before and after my removal to Austria. 2nd, Because he had to account to me for many things in Augsburg. Our correspondence touched, indeed, on some delicate points, but, at all events, it did no injury.to the Austrian state or to religion.

"My seventh correspondent was J. WEINHOFER, vice-archdeacon at Pinkafield, in Hungary, a very pious, conscientious man, who had long been in correspondence with professor Sailer; but not having obtained satisfaction from his books and letters, in 1811, requested permission to visit him. To this Sailer consented, but wished him, on his way through Lintz, to call on me at Gallneukirch, and open his anxieties to me. Weinhofer called on me most unexpectedly, in May, told me of Sailer's recommendation, and laid open the state of his mind. God quieted and purified his heart by faith in Christ, and after spending some days with me, he returned home peaceful, thankful, and joyful, and postponed his journey to Landshut. What could be more natural than that he should often write to me of matters relating to faith and conscience, and seek further comfort and advice from me respecting the salvation that is in Christ? But we could both declare upon oath that we never thought of a secret association."

Boos then mentions other correspondents; the baron Grumpenberg, a Bavarian by birth —baron Rufin, also of Bavaria—Anna Schlatter, whose name has already occurred in this narrative—Maria Oberdorfer, by birth a Lutheran—bishop Sailer's secretary—and Gallus Poggo, prefect of the Catholic Seminary at St. Gall.

Lastly, he refers to a person of the name of Grellet, who had been deputed by some Christians in North America to visit Sailer and his disciples, in whose efforts to diffuse spiritual Christianity in the Romish church they took a deep interest. He had, however, no direct intercourse with Boos; for, having heard that neither he nor any other person in Gallneu-kirch understood either French or English, he merely sent a message to say that he felt most closely allied to him in spirit. He returned home by way of Nuremburg and Amsterdam; and having informed his friends in those places of the particulars of his visit, they collected six hundred florins, which were transmitted to Munich, with a request that Sailer and Boos would distribute them among the most needy persons in their connexion as they might think fit. Of this sum, however, none passed through Boos's hands, though he was informed that two-thirds of it was spent in charity, and the rest appropriated to publishing an edition of the New Testament.

CHAPTER XIX.

Answers to objections—The Bishop's injunction—The Emperor's decision—Boos's departure from Austria.

DURING the proceedings against Boos at this time, it was said, that these religious awakenings were mere illusion and self-deception. To which he answered:—

"What proceeds from illusion and imagination is of short duration. But this awakening, this joy and peace in the Holy Ghost, through faith in Christ, has lasted with me and many hundreds of others, for twenty-five years—from 1790 in Kempten, to 1815 in Gallneukirch. There must, consequently, be truth and reality, and something Divine about it; for it is not conceivable that hundreds and thousands of individuals should deceive themselves for such a length of time together, particularly since this illusion, as it is called, has been all the while so constantly calumniated and persecuted. Mere illusion is soon gone, and will not stand a twenty-five years' trial.

"Paul, on his way to Damascus, was surrounded by a heavenly light, and, by the Lord's appearance and voice, was suddenly changed

from a wolf into a lamb. He was afterwards
caught up into the third heaven, where he
heard unutterable words; and frequently the
Lord or an angel appeared to him in the night,
and spoke to him.   Was that also an illusion?
Cold reason, inexperienced in Divine things,
says, indeed, with Festus, 'Paul, thou art deluded! thou art beside thyself' (Acts xxvi. 24).
But faith replies, 'I am not deluded, most noble
Festus, but speak the words of truth and sober-
ness.   The king knoweth of these things.
King Agrippa, believest thou this ?'

"Alderman Höllinger, in Gallneukirch, five
years ago, as everybody knows, was furious,
like Saul, against Boos and the faith which he
preached. But on Trinity Sunday, (in the year
1810,) while reading the passage in Rom. ix.
30—33, a heavenly light shone suddenly into
his soul.   'From being a Saul,' said he, 'I
became a Paul; I saw clearly that the clergyman was in the right, and that I was in the
wrong.'   With the Bible in his hand, he ran to
me weeping, entreated my forgiveness before
witnesses for all his calumnies against me, and
has been ever since that time a most zealous
defender of his pastor and the truth.   Let any
one tell this aged and pious man, that his faith
and light are an illusion, and hear what reply
he will make ! . . . .

"Christ is still carrying on the work which
he began when he was on earth, in converting
and saving men.   Our awakenings are like
those which He himself effected in Zaccheus,

Matthew, Peter, Paul, Nicodemus, the Samaritan woman at Jacob's well, Mary Magdalene, the man that was born blind, etc.; and like those effected by the apostles and their companions on the day of Pentecost, and in the instances of the Philippian jailer, Lydia, Cornelius, etc. Our awakened people have heard and received the same gospel with the same joy and thankfulness, as glad tidings which they had never heard before; and have walked in newness of life. . . . .

" Our awakened people were formerly poor in spirit, mourning for their sins, hungering and thirsting after righteousness. Now we know that of such it is said, ' Theirs is the kingdom of heaven :' and when the gospel is preached to such, it is always effectual, and must be so. Is it likely that the most humble, the most zealous, and the most pious people in the whole parish should be deluded, and that the proud and ungodly should alone have the true light ?

" These awakenings have produced the most delightful fruits of virtue and godliness. Persons, for example, who formerly stole, gambled, and lived riotously, now do so no more. Many who formerly dreaded God like slaves, now love Him as children; and many who formerly neither read nor understood the Bible, now read and understand it with joy. Are these good fruits the effects of an illusion ? Would that the whole world were thus deluded ! Such illusions would neither be injurious to the government nor to the church, even were they secret. But they are made public enough." . . . .

Another reproach against Boos and his friends is thus referred to by him in a letter:—

"It was said, in the presence of the consistory, that our holy cause was a mere woman's matter. My answer was,

"*First*, it is not true; for there are hundreds of men besides, and among them men who are known to the world as professors, authors, presidents, deans, clergymen, barons, etc.

"But, *secondly*, if women, children, and simple-minded people attain sooner and more frequently to a vital knowledge of Jesus Christ, the reason is,

" 1. Because Christ has promised them that it should be so, (Matt. xi. 25.)

" 2. Because, according to Paul, (1 Cor. i. 26,) not many wise, not many noble, are called ; but, on the contrary, there were among the first Christians many that were unlearned and despised.

" 3. Because women and simple-hearted people do not, like the learned, seek to make holy things comprehensible to their acute understandings ; but receive the truth with the heart, with good-will, and faith ; and when the heart is purified by faith, (Acts xv. 9,) they are then able to contemplate and to know God, and Christ, and Divine things, better than Socrates himself.

" 4. Pious persons of the female sex have,

from ancient times, generally sought God earlier, more frequently, and with a more filial and earnest spirit than the men; and 'he that seeketh, findeth.'

" 5. The great mysteries of the conception, birth, and resurrection of Christ were first revealed to women. Why is not Christ ashamed of commencing such great things with women? Why did he even reprove the eleven for not believing the women, who saw him first after his resurrection? Why did Christ begin to establish his faith and his kingdom in Samaria by means of a woman—a sinful woman? and Paul the church at Philippi by Lydia?

" 6. It is said that 'the just shall live by faith,'—not by understanding or reason. But women can believe as well as men, or better."

Such was the determined animosity of Boos's adversaries, that they left no expedient untried to fix crimes upon him of which he was perfectly innocent, or to induce him to renounce his religious principles. One day, the bishop of Lintz visited him in prison, and urged him to retract his doctrines. Boos, in reply, made a powerful appeal to his conscience, and asked him how he could attempt to make him deny the truth. The bishop was so irritated as to spit in his face, and rushed out of the prison, with a determination to wreak his vengeance upon him. Accordingly, on the 16th of February, 1816, an injunction came, signed by the bishop and his chancellor, stating that as the authorities had obtained information that several of Boos's parishioners had visited and conversed with him, (in violation of the order which had been made when he entered the convent of the Carmelites as a prisoner,) he must in future be kept in close custody, and not be allowed to perform mass till further orders.

Boos from this time was subjected to the most rigorous inspection. Hitherto he had occasionally taken walks beyond his narrow cell and breathed the fresh air. But this favour was now denied him. He never saw any human being excepting his jailor's servant.

"Blessed are ye," said our Lord to his disciples, "when men shall revile you, and persecute you, and shall say all manner of evil against you falsely, for my sake. Rejoice, and be exceeding glad : for great is your reward in heaven : for so persecuted they the prophets that were before you." These words comforted Boos's mind. He was refreshed by the thought that he was suffering for his attachment to that Saviour who had "endured the contradiction of sinners against himself."

But the end of his captivity was approaching. A soldier, whom the captain before mentioned had given him to wait on him, took a lively interest in his welfare ; and, one Sunday morning, when he brought the minister's frugal repast, he said, "I have heard good news. The prior has told me that you will soon be set at liberty." "How is that ? Has the decision of the court been received ?" "Probably ;

though the prior did not tell me positively. For the first time he asked me how you were. I told him that you were far from well; and that your extreme weakness obliged you to keep your bed. Upon this the prior told me that he would obtain permission for you to walk in the corridor."—More than six weeks, however, passed between this conversation and his release; and during this interval, he was always watched with the same strictness. He was not allowed to take any walks or to receive visitors; and, in short, experienced no alleviation of his captivity.

The emperor at last pronounced the sentence. It was to the effect that, though Boos was perfectly innocent of the charge of belonging to any secret society, he was to be detained till the archbishop of Vienna should judge him worthy of being set at liberty; but in no case was he to reside in the diocese of Lintz: he might perform his clerical functions elsewhere; and if he requested to leave the country, permission would be granted.

Such was the result of this long investigation. Boos was acknowledged to be innocent, but he had given offence to his diocesan, and therefore must be treated as if guilty. If guilty, he should have been convicted and punished; if innocent, he should have been restored to his parish—his full acquittal should have been publicly announced, and his calumniators been exposed. But no; his enemies wished to get rid of a scriptural preacher, and chase him from Austria; and in this they succeeded.

Boos did not avail himself of the offer to give him another appointment elsewhere. He requested his passport, and on the 30th of May left Lintz for his native country, Bavaria. His departure was lamented by multitudes in Austria, to whom he had been made a blessing. The government allowed him a thousand florins for his travelling expenses; but would not permit him to return to Gallneukirch, to take leave of his four thousand parishioners, and to arrange his affairs. His goods were sold by auction; and, after several deductions, the balance was remitted to him.

On the 1st of June he reached Munich; it was Whitsuntide eve. Some of his friends had assembled to celebrate the festival when he knocked at the door. On opening it, a stranger presented himself, pale, emaciated, and bearing all the marks of extreme suffering. They did not recognise him till he exclaimed, "What! do you not know me?" when they rushed into his arms. How great was the joy of his brethren in the faith to behold once more their long-tried and much-beloved friend! The joy of those, too, was scarcely less, who saw him now for the first time. His heart and his lips overflowed with gratitude and love, as he related the blessings and the sufferings he had experienced in Austria.

CHAPTER XX.

Boos a private tutor at Weihern—Professor at Dusseldorf—
Minister at Sayn.

Boos stayed only nine days at Munich. At the end of that time, not being able to obtain a parish on account of the prejudices which had been raised against him even in his own country, he entered as private tutor into a respectable family at Weihern, some leagues from the city. He had the charge of educating two children; one eight, the other thirteen years old. This employment was, we may suppose, not very congenial, for he speaks of it as "a dry occupation." Yet it seems to have given him at first some relief from the turmoil and agitation of public life. He even expressed to a friend his thankfulness that God enabled him to live as contented while so engaged, as if he had converted, or silenced, half the world.

But "this is not your rest," was still to be the motto of his life. In December, 1816, he was summoned before the provincial court, and ordered to leave the country within four and twenty hours, or three days at the farthest. Astonished at this proceeding, he repaired immediately to Munich, and endeavoured to learn from the authorities for what reason he was to be banished from his native country. "Because you have been accused," he was informed, "of being at the head of a dangerous society of mystics." " If that be mysticism," he boldly replied, " which the Lord Jesus, and the apostles Peter and John preached, I acknowledge that I am a mystic, for I have always aimed at teaching what they taught." " We shall be well pleased," they said, " if you can clear yourself from the charges brought against you by three consistories." " I will attempt it," Boos replied; " I only request a revocation of the order for my banishment, and a longer respite." This was granted ; the uncle of his pupils likewise interceded in his favour ; and by the efforts of some other influential persons, he was allowed to remain unmolested.

The following are a few extracts from Boos's letters during this period:—

"Munich, 4th June, 1816.—I look back with tears on the forlorn four thousand at Gallneukirch.* May God preserve and keep them ! They have been stedfast in the faith thus far. But now efforts are made to turn them from light to darkness, to take their New Testaments from them, etc. Pray for them."

* When Boos's successor, Brunner, was installed at Gallneukirch, not more than ten of the parishioners came to give him the right hand of fellowship, according to the custom of that country. The four thousand were four times called upon by the dean to go to the altar, and give their hands to the new vicar, and swear fidelity and obedience to him ; but they would not go, or stretch out a hand.

" Weihern, January, 1817.—With my flock in Austria, I have only an *invisible* connexion, because all visible correspondence is intercepted. They have taken away all Höchstetter's letters and books, because they imagine he preserves the four thousand in the faith. After severely persecuting Leopold they have banished him to a remote part of Hungary; and I can no longer hear from him . . . . Yet the knowledge of the Lord is increasing around us, though I am compelled to stand idle. Gossner, Lindl, and many others are going forwards, and daily making new disciples."

" Weihern, 19th March, 1817.—A few days ago, my brother, the cross manufacturer at Augsburg, called on me. On asking him how things were going on, he said, ' Miserably ! no one will buy a cross now-a-days.' 'I believe it,' was my answer, ' for every one is already provided with them. I for one will not be a customer to you.' "

In the spring of 1817, a severe illness brought him apparently to the brink of the grave, in which, however, he experienced such an assurance of his salvation, through a living faith in Christ, and such a joyful willingness to die, that he wished his faith might frequently be thus re-animated, though it were by the recurrence of such attacks. His recovery was slow and imperfect. But he longed for a wider sphere of activity; and his wishes were unexpectedly granted by an invitation from the Prussian government to become professor and

catechist in the Gymnasium at Dusseldorf, on
the Rhine ; which, as there appeared no hope
of his being again allowed to preach in Bavaria,
he gladly accepted.

On the 12th of October, 1817, he took leave
of his friends at Weihern, and proceeded to
his new appointment. His duties were to give
religious instruction to all the classes, and to
teach the principles of the Latin language. He
was also to be allowed to preach after being
duly installed. He had scarcely commenced
his labours, when he was summoned to attend
the vicar-general's court at Cologne. He went,
(as he expresses it) like a burnt child who
dreads the fire; but was agreeably surprised at
the reception he met with. Instead of a long
and rigorous examination, which he had been
led to expect, when De Caspars, the vicar-
general, entered the room, he asked Boos
whether he had already filled the pastoral
office. He answered that he had filled it so
long that he had lost every hair of his head
in it. On this the vicar-general laughed, and
after looking over his testimonials, assented to
his admission into the diocese.

The general character of the students in the
Gymnasium afforded him little satisfaction.
With scarcely an exception, they were wild and
reckless, and hardened against religious impressions. Yet after labouring among them for
some months he was gratified by the desire
they manifested to obtain copies of the Scriptures. " The students, both lay and ecclesias-

tical," he says, "appear becoming more hungry for the Word of Life, and have already taken forty copies. The students who seemed formerly to dread the Bible more than the devil, show just now great confidence in the Munich edition, after seeing the archbishop's approval of it."

In February, 1819, the magistrates, with the approbation of the episcopal council at Ehren-breitstein, offered him the country parish of Sayn, a village on the Rhine, between Coblentz and Neuwied. He very readily gave up his professorship, and returned to those pastoral duties in which he had spent the greater part of his life, and ardently longed to spend his remaining days. He removed to Sayn in June, 1819, and continued there till his death.

In this, as in every other place, he found it to be true that "they who will live godly in Christ Jesus, must suffer persecution." The neighbouring clergy regarded with distrust a preacher who exalted the name of Christ above that of the Virgin Mary and the saints, and who insisted so forcibly on the necessity of the regeneration of the heart. Some of the literary journals attacked Boos and his so-called heresies with great virulence. The vicar-general at length felt compelled to address a circular to all the clergy in his diocese, in which Boos was instructed to abstain from all confidential inter-course with persons of other communions, to avoid singularity, and to submit his discourses to his clerical brethren.

Three years later, the vicar-general wrote to Boos, and expressed his regret that, in a pastoral letter of the bishop of Augsburg, and in some other publications, he was mentioned as the leader of the spurious mystics; and called upon him to renounce all participation in such views, and to declare that he adhered to the true principles of the Catholic church.

"That which is spurious," said Boos, "I can renounce with a safe conscience, when I am called upon to do it. I therefore made a solemn declaration to that effect, but with the express addition, that if by a spurious mysticism was intended the pure, ancient, apostolic faith which I had always preached, I must retract this declaration. With this the vicar-general expressed himself perfectly satisfied. . . . . If by a spurious mysticism be understood a dangerous secret association which threatens equally church and state, who would not at once declare against it, and reject it with abhorrence ?"

The labours of Boos at Sayn were far from being so successful as they had been in Austria. Writing to his friend Gossner, he says, "You must come to me that these bean-eaters may be brought to a knowledge of the truth. I can make no impression on them; for they spend their Sundays in dancing and dram-drinking. I see no end to my misery, for they are all gross and selfish. My soul is greatly troubled; I sigh and cry to the Lord, but he answers me not; and if I preach to them as I have been wont, these boors neither understand nor hear me."

A Christian traveller passing through Sayn called on Boos, and gives the following account of his visit:—"One of the most interesting occurrences in my whole journey was a visit I paid to that man of God, Martin Boos. He dwells in what was once a convent, or rather in a house that was contiguous to it, for the convent itself is in ruins. The good old man happened to be in his garden when we arrived. We were conducted into a large and lofty apartment of the old monastery, which was very partially fitted up with his little stock of furniture. He soon came in, bade us welcome, and set wine and bread before us. One could not but look at such a man with reverence, who had endured so many sufferings for Christ and his name. He is now bent down with age and infirmities. He has had two paralytic attacks, which have deprived him of the use of his right side. He is still the object of many slanderous attacks, against which he is obliged to defend himself. But he is most of all dejected on account of the want of success in his labours. 'Oh, how happy,' said he, ' was I in Austria! For two years I fought and wrestled in the anguish of my heart on account of my sins. Whatever time I could spare by day and night, I prostrated myself in the church before the altar, and half my congregation were in anguish on account of their sins, until light sprang up in my own mind, and I was enabled to comfort both them and myself. But *here*, not a soul mourns for his sins. If an anxious sinner applies to me, he comes from a distance; but here no one turns to God. They live in sinful pleasure, and wish to remain so!'"

Besides his intercourse with his own parishioners, Boos was visited at Sayn by a great number of pious people travelling up and down the Rhine, many of whom derived much benefit from hearing him relate his own eventful history, and from opening their hearts to him, and were comforted, instructed, and strengthened in faith.

Multitudes of pilgrims, also, who every year flocked to that place, came to Boos to make confession ; and he let none of them depart without endeavouring to lodge in their hearts seeds of Divine truth, by which they might, sooner or later, be drawn to the Saviour.

Towards the end of his life, the fruits of his labours in Sayn began to appear; and thus the promise was fulfilled, that "in due season we shall reap, if we faint not." It became evident that he had not prayed, laboured, and suffered in vain, in this apparently barren and ungrateful soil. Boos himself had the happiness to see some blessed fruits, and others saw still more. But most are seen by that eye which surveys all lands, and looks into every heart.

CHAPTER XXI.

Boos's last days.

AFTER he had been a few years at Sayn, Boos's health began to decline rapidly. Finding himself unequal to the discharge of his regular duties, he wished to obtain the assistance of his friend Gossner, to whom he thus wrote:—

"Sayn, June 4, 1824.—My mental and physical powers are daily getting weaker, yet I drag myself along, and preach on Sundays and holidays without assistance." . . . .

"June 10.—I am living with one foot in the grave. I can scarcely do anything from a failure of strength, in body, soul, and spirit; and hence I have been thinking either of giving up my charge, and retiring altogether from clerical duties, or obtaining an assistant, or, if it were possible, requesting you to come to me. My parishioners would welcome you. . . . . If you could arrange your affairs elsewhere, we might rest, labour, suffer, believe, and die together in this sequestered spot. . . . I would willingly sacrifice the repose I have hitherto had here, for it is the wish of my heart to see another religious awakening, and then die. For I must confess to my shame, that not a single soul has yet been awakened; and hence arises

my outward tranquillity.   Yet I am not at rest
either outwardly or inwardly.   Anonymous
scribblers still abuse me as a heretic, as they
do you.   My insensible parishioners are the
grief of my heart, and those who are said to be
awakened, are full of complaints."

Gossner, however, could not comply with his
friend's invitation.   Having been forced to
quit Bavaria on account of his alleged heresy,
he settled in Poland, where all the power of
the emperor Alexander was not sufficient to
preserve him from being harassed by the clergy.

About this period Boos passed through a
crisis in his health which was the forerunner
of his dissolution.   "Since Martinmas," he
writes to Gossner, on January 15, 1825, "the
Lord has thrown me into a mortar, and
pounded me like bread-corn.   For fourteen
days I suffered from violent cramp in the
stomach, then from inflammation of the lungs.
To save time the medical man opened a vein
with his penknife, and the bandage getting
loose without my being aware, I lost an immense quantity of blood.   This was followed
by dropsy, affecting both my body and feet.
Twice the surgeon has reduced the dropsy,
but it continually threatens to return.   My
whole body has been covered with blisters,
mustard poultices, and leeches.   By this treatment I was brought so low, that for ten weeks
I could not stir a step.   I quite lost my appetite.
I made application for a curate, but none was
sent me.   For the last three days, however,

the Lord has granted me some amendment. My appetite has returned; the dropsy keeps off; and I can write these lines, though with much debility and effort. Before the new year began, I had given up all hopes of recovery, and thought of nothing but dying. I received the sacrament for the last time, asked forgiveness of my parishioners, and made my will. In every house and in the church prayers were offered for me; and my parishioners evinced more love and regard for me than I had believed they possessed. Every day they surrounded my bed and wept."

On the 9th of February he wrote again to the same friend:—" I am a little better, but still so weak that I am incapable of serving either God or man. . . .

" A few days ago, the bishop sent me a Royal Ordinance by which the king* guarantees one hundred florins yearly to my church, for the expenses of public worship; twenty-four dollars to my sacristan; three hundred and twenty dollars to my successor; and to me, for my life, a thousand florins, with the use of the real property. Lastly, he presents my congregation with the old bishop's palace, for a school-house, and a residence for the sacristan. Many persons advise me to resign, and enjoy my income in peace. But I dread inactivity more than death."

"February 28.—Since my last letter, I am

---

* That is, the king of Prussia, in whose dominions Boos was now living.

become not stronger, but weaker, so that I can scarcely hold a pen. . . . Oh that you were with me! I have no one here to comfort me under my extreme sufferings. All that I have endured heretofore is as nothing compared with what I now suffer. My faith is often exposed to violent assaults. Yet the Lord, after a dreadful day, has granted me a quiet night, and comforted me while thus preparing for death with the following considerations:—

" 1. Behold! now thou art on the threshold of eternity, like a beggar, with a wallet full of sins, deserving nought but the punishment of hell.

" 2. The good works thou hast performed in this life are God's gifts and graces, but defiled by thy self-love. If I were now permitted and enabled to preach, and to perform other services for the honour of God and the salvation of men, what a favour would this be! If, therefore, God rewards what is good in me, he rewards his own gifts, but which I have defiled. How poor am I in thy sight, O God!

" 3. The trials I endured in Bavaria and Austria on account of Christ and the gospel were partly gifts of God, partly necessary and wholesome chastisement, in which God will find little or nothing to reward. In short, I have nothing meritorious before God.

" 4. My patience and my resignation in my last illness were often weak. How poor am I therefore to the end of my life, before thee, O God! I possess and desire nothing but what was granted to the thief on the cross, and to Zaccheus. If I do not obtain this, it will fare ill with me.

"I am therefore forced to grasp *that* with all my might, for which men have abhorred me as a heretic, and persecuted me even to this day. . . . Pray for me, that I may not suffer shipwreck of faith, and that the Lord may pardon me, if I have kept silence, from the fear of man."

A few days later, he wrote as follows :—

"Alas! what do I hear of the believers in Gallneukirch ? They are vilified and persecuted in such a manner, that they wish to go over.* They will be driven out of the church by the blind bigots. . . . . These are perhaps the last lines I shall ever write to you. I thank you for all your love. Pardon all I have done amiss; and pray for your fellow-pilgrim, who is dying in the greatest enjoyment of the faith. . . . .

"In this dying state I cannot but feel astonished beyond measure, that the heads of our church condemn precisely what comforts me on my death-bed, and that my clerical brethren do nothing now to comfort me, but totally forsake me. . . . . . We need exactly such a Christ when we are dying, as we preach while we are living. May he help us both! . . . . In and at death this is my confession of faith—Faith that worketh by love, justifies and saves us here and hereafter. If this is yours

---

* Namely, to the Lutheran church.

also, you are one with Paul and James, and with your dying Zobo" (Boos.)

The last letter Boos ever wrote was addressed to the same friend, and is dated June 15, 1825. " You will not believe that I am dying, because I have so often told you that I was, and yet am not dead. However, I am treading on the very edge of the grave with my thick, swollen feet, and may fall into it to-day or to-morrow; whence Jesus, the resurrection and the life, will raise me on 'that day.' I wrote to you yesterday, to return you my hearty thanks for the second part of your ' *Spiritual Casket*,'* by means of which the Lord has inexpressibly comforted, revived, and cheered me. For a very long time, as I complained to you, my body and soul were full of poison, mercury, gall, bitterness, discomfort, distrust, and unbelief, as if they were possessed with seven devils ; but when, on the 5th of June, your ' *Casket*' was brought in by a shoemaker as I lay in bed, and I began to read it, the seven devils were expelled ; heart and eyes swam with tears, and peace and joy in the Holy Ghost returned to a degree beyond expression. . . . . I was also very glad that, in that work, you enjoined and enforced holiness and righteousness of life, as much as the righteousness of faith, and thus relieved me from the fear that you were one-sided. For I find in dying that we must 'follow after holiness' in

---

* A work by Gossner, consisting of short meditations on texts of Scripture for every day in the year.

order to be fit for the land of the holy. 'Without holiness,'—without having his robes washed and made pure in the blood of the Lamb,—'no man shall see the Lord.' " . . .

An account of the last days of this good man has been given by a friend who was with him to the close. " During the last two months he suffered extremely, in part through the treatment of the physician, and in part from the state of his own mind, in which for a time the clear and believing view of his Lord and Saviour which he usually enjoyed, was obscured. He was tried in the furnace, that the trial of his faith might be found more precious than gold seven times purified. But soon his heart overflowed with the warmest gratitude, and the enjoyments of grace. When I visited him, I found him weak, and suffering dreadfully from the dropsy, but his mind was cheerful and serene in the firm faith that he had obtained grace and the forgiveness of sins, not for his own merits, but only through the blood and merits of Jesus Christ, and that now he should go home in peace."

One of his friends, Anna Jacobi, hearing of his lonely condition, and that he was destitute of those human helps and comforts which his afflicted state needed, immediately repaired to Sayn and spent several days with him. She writes —" His conversation and the full confidence he manifested in the Saviour as able to supply all his need, made a very deep and salutary impression on me. I afterwards repeated my visit, and remained a fortnight by his bed-side. I had never before enjoyed the privilege of being at the bed-side of a true Christian, and hearing him converse freely on the present and the future. . . . I found him very weak and suffering much bodily pain and great oppression in the chest, with loss of sleep and appetite. . . . When he felt himself rather more at ease, he was cheerful, and even lively. He would then narrate many very interesting passages in his life. . . . On the 14th of July I returned home ; and after that he lived six weeks. Some days after my departure a young man from C. called upon him; having no pressing engagement, and seeing how much the venerable man needed assistance, he offered to remain with him and nurse him. This office he performed with much affection and fidelity to the period of his decease. On August 10th Boos dictated his last letter to me, in which he took leave of us. After alluding to his approaching end, he added, ' I would gladly take leave by letter of my teacher, SAILER, but as I am unable, I beg that you will thank him in my stead for his instructions and exertions by which he taught me in my youth to know the Father and the Son, and thus to find everlasting life. Thank him too, for his love, help, advice, and consolations in my sufferings and tribulations. I entreat also his forgiveness for all the trouble which, without intending it, I have occasioned him in this life. The venerable bishop Homer has also protected me to the end of my life;

and the other clergy have treated me with love
and esteem, for which I return them my thanks
with hearty benediction, on leaving this world.'"
This letter was subscribed by himself.

"On the 29th of August, ten minutes before
five in the afternoon, he died, after a short
struggle, gently and quietly, having uttered the
words, 'Lord Jesus, into thy hands I commend
my spirit.'"

Such was the death of this remarkable man.
His whole life had been a succession of sufferings and persecutions, while he never ceased
to proclaim the great salvation with un-
daunted courage, in a manner peculiarly forcible
and original. God leads extraordinary men
through extraordinary ways, which common
persons, even though pious, cannot understand.

The friend in whose arms he died, caused a
simple wooden cross to be placed over his
grave, with the inscription:—

Here rests the Reverend MARTIN BOOS, aged 63.
He died in the Lord. Rev. xiv. 13.

The glen in which he found a grave, and
probably those who prepared it and placed his
remains in it, knew not what kind of man he
was; but at the resurrection, when it will
" appear what we shall be," his true character
will be manifested; for then the righteous shall
" shine as the brightness of the firmament; and
they that turn many to righteousness as the
stars, for ever and ever," (Dan. xii. 3.)

CHAPTER XXII.

Sketch of Boos's character and labours—Concluding remarks.

THE following brief sketch of Boos's character and labours is contained in a letter which has been received from the Rev. JOHANNES GOSSNER, while the foregoing pages have been passing through the press:—

"Through the agency of Boos, numbers beyond calculation in the Roman Catholic church, both clergy and laity, were awakened, enlightened, and converted; many of whom are still to this day continuing to live and labour for the Lord, and in whose labours he still lives. He was indeed a real reformer; not so much, it is true, from without, by introducing a new form, but *in* the Roman Catholic church, by awakening and confirming faith in *Christ for us and in us* . . . . . I am convinced that he was the instrument in the hand of the Lord of awakening and spreading a true life of faith in Germany. The Lord placed him as a light on a candlestick, at which thousands lighted their dim or expiring lamp. He did not want to shine; and for this very reason his flame burned the brighter. Oh that you had known him — the simple, plain, modest

man, who had no confidence in himself;—
but when from the pulpit he sounded his
trumpet he was like a lion; and in conversation he burned and flamed like a torch ; and
then, as if he were nothing, he hastened to retire
to his closet, and there, the whole night through,
watched and prayed for the outpouring of the
Holy Spirit, because he knew it was not he that
wrought, but that it was only the Holy Spirit,
who, in and through him, could give light and
life, and lead into all truth."

In reviewing this narrative, it will appear to
many surprising, that a man who so firmly
held, and so faithfully preached, the great truths
of the gospel, should have continued to the end
of his life in the Roman Catholic church. That
he was conscientious in doing so, is proved, not
only by his whole character and conduct, but
also by the fact, that he might, by leaving the
Romish church, and entering one of the Protestant churches of Germany, not only have
passed his life in peace, but have attained an
object still dearer to his heart—that of preaching the gospel freely and without molestation.
Two of his fellow-labourers and sharers in his
afflictions, Gossner and Lindl, carrying out
their principles to their legitimate results, openly
embraced the Protestant faith ; and the former
of them has for many years laboured with
great success as pastor of the Bohemian church
at Berlin. A considerable number, also, of

Boos's converts in Austria, after his banishment from them, finding that they must either relinquish their obedience to Christ, or renounce their allegiance to the Romish church, chose the better path ; and, after for a time enduring great trials, and severe assaults upon their faith,* they at last obtained permission from the government to form a Protestant congregation, and to worship God according to their consciences.   How, then, was it that one who really held so many Protestant principles, who was such a lover of his Lord and of his word, should still have remained in a church which has departed so widely from the Scriptures, and from whose tyrannous and persecuting spirit he was himself so great a sufferer ?

Much may doubtless be ascribed to the influence of education and early association, which made him unwilling to abandon a church in which (as he says in a letter, written near the close of his life) he had been " born and bred, and had been bedewed with the influences of grace, and of the knowledge of Christ:" though (as he further states in the same letter) he saw much in her with which he was displeased ; and the severe persecutions with which she had visited him for preaching the doctrine of justification by faith, had caused the most painful struggles in his mind.   But he was unwilling on that account, unless he

* The celebrated prince Hohenloe visited them, and endeavoured to prevail upon them to return to the Roman Catholic church, but in vain.

were cast out, to take a step which he thought would offend and grieve many; considering (as he goes on to say) that there was a mixture of wheat and tares in every church, and that vital Christianity is misunderstood and persecuted in all communities, and in all countries. Boos was also, no doubt, influenced by the great usefulness of his labours among his people; and by the enjoyment of Christian fellowship among the little circle of like-minded men with whom he communicated, either personally or by letter. But, probably, the circumstance which, above all others, operated to prevent his leaving the communion in which he had been brought up, was the state and character of the Protestant churches around him, at that period; which were, for the most part, under the withering influence of a neology nearly approaching to infidelity, or of a cold, heartless orthodoxy. So that Lutheranism was associated in his mind (as appears from some of his letters) with laxity in faith and in practice; and such was the general condition of the Protestant congregations in Austria and Bavaria at that time, that there was probably not one of them which could number so many sincere believers as Boos's at Gallneukirch. There has happily been a considerable improvement, of late years, in the religious state of the Protestants in that part of the continent; though, alas! they are yet, as a body, far from being worthy successors of the German Reformers.

While, however these considerations explain,

in some measure, the course pursued by Boos, it must not be overlooked that such a line of conduct appears inconsistent with the solemn call and warning: "Come out of her, my people, that ye be not partakers of her sins, and that ye receive not of her plagues." (Rev. xviii. 4.

It is deeply interesting to see how God was pleased to make the pure light of His gospel to shine in the midst of Romish darkness, notwithstanding all the efforts of adversaries to extinguish it; and how powerfully it operated in attracting some and offending others. For the gospel is still, as in the days of Paul, either " the savour of life unto life," or " of death unto death," (2 Cor. ii. 16.) This short history also presents a resemblance, on a small scale, to the great scenes of the Reformation. The treatment which Boos experienced from the Romish church was that which those who preached the same doctrines three centuries before had endured. This persecution, however, was remarkably overruled for the furtherance of the gospel: since those doctrines which, had they been allowed to be taught without opposition, might perhaps not have extended beyond a few villages in Suabia, were, in consequence of the efforts made to suppress them, diffused through a great part of Catholic Germany.

THE RELIGIOUS TRACT SOCIETY: INSTITUTED 1799.